Prais

Closer Tha

"Warning: Susan Hill has written a deceptive book. It looks like another woman-with-a-fragile-marriage-struggles-in-her-relationship-with-God book. Yet her life and spiritual experiences become compellingly honest and transparent."

— CECIL MURPHEY, coauthor of *90 Minutes in Heaven,*
Heaven Is Real, and more than 100 other books

"Over the last sixty years I have read numerous works on Christian spirituality. But I must say that Susan Hill has made the best case I've ever read for intimacy with God. It is biblically sound, psychologically real and personally honest. I've never heard any theologian or Bible teacher portray as powerfully as Susan does the true intimacy with God as Jesus promises in the relation of the branch and the vine (John 15:1–9). I think this is the book that millions of Christians have been waiting for!"

— JAMES W. THARP, founder and president of Christian
Renewal Ministries and author of *Revival Must Come!*
and *The Spirit of Prayer*

"Susan's book will lead the reader on an interesting journey of discovery and clarification. She is right about life with God being adventurous and breathtaking. Writing with a vulnerability that allows the light of God's grace to shine through real life situations, she presents God's way as both beneficial and desirable. She leads us through her ideas with anticipation. It will help people clarify the real issue of living with God. I read it for interest and edification, and I was not disappointed."

— DUDLEY HALL, founder and president of Successful
Christian Living Ministries

"Some books argue that God exists. This book gives us His address. Some books tell us about Him, this book shows us what He looks like. If you've ever wondered if there's more to the Christian life, Susan Hill doesn't just assure us that there is, she hands us a roadmap and shows us how to get there."

—PHIL CALLAWAY, popular speaker and best-selling author

"As a Christian, my journey with God often seems more like working for a demanding employer than walking hand in hand with my first love. Susan Hill's book was a refreshing reminder that it is the latter and not the former that the Lord desires of me. Her stories take you to the feet of the Father of Love to encounter His incredible kindness for yourself. I hope as you read this book you too can discover why the 'nearness of God is [our] good.' (Psalm 73:28)"

—JIMMY NEEDHAM, recording artist, Inpop Records

Closer Than Your Skin

Closer Than Your Skin

Unwrapping the Mystery of Intimacy with God

Susan D. Hill

WATERBROOK
PRESS

CLOSER THAN YOUR SKIN
PUBLISHED BY WATERBROOK PRESS
12265 Oracle Boulevard, Suite 200
Colorado Springs, Colorado 80921
A division of Random House Inc.

All Scripture quotations, unless otherwise indicated, are taken from the New American Standard Bible®. © Copyright The Lockman Foundation 1960, 1962, 1963, 1968, 1971, 1972, 1973, 1975, 1977, 1995. Used by permission. (www.Lockman.org). Scripture quotations marked (NIV) are taken from the Holy Bible, New International Version®. NIV®. Copyright © 1973, 1978, 1984 by International Bible Society. Used by permission of Zondervan Publishing House. All rights reserved.

Italics in Scripture quotations reflect the author's added emphasis.

Details in some anecdotes and stories have been changed to protect the identities of the persons involved.

ISBN 978-1-4000-7382-5

Library of Congress Cataloging-in-Publication Data
Hill, Susan D.
   Closer than your skin : unwrapping the mystery of intimacy with God / Susan D. Hill. — 1st ed.
         p. cm.
   Includes bibliographical references.
   ISBN 978-1-4000-7382-5
 1. Spirituality. I. Title.
   BV4501.3.H553 2007
   248.4—dc22

                              2007039317

Printed in the United States of America
2008

10 9 8 7 6 5 4 3

To Duncan
Because you were hungry and thirsty for
more of God

It's worth it brothers
It's worth it friends
To know your maker
To lose your sin
Did you know that you are dearly loved?

No greater joy
No greater peace
No greater love than this

—JIMMY NEEDHAM, "DEARLY LOVED"

Contents

Why I Wrote This Book

*The biggest human temptation is
to settle for too little.*

—THOMAS MERTON

In 1985, after seven years of marriage, my husband, Duncan, had become a full-blown alcoholic. Then my world exploded when I discovered he was also having an affair. Pregnant with our second daughter, I was already emotionally volatile. But now, day after day, I secretly wept in the shower of our newly built home that overlooked the Gallatin Valley. Although Duncan eventually quit drinking, ended the affair, and started attending Alcoholics Anonymous, our marriage remained fragile. Sobriety was tough, but adding a baby to the turmoil stretched our sanity paper thin.

The tension grew unbearable. I felt stung by his betrayal and reacted with hot flashes of anger. I started checking his whereabouts, the phone bill, and his wallet. Trust was shattered, and the deep hole of sorrow sucked me into its gloominess. My wrestling mind asked all the whys and what ifs that follow a loss. In time, I grew weary of the pain. I longed to overcome my emotions and return to some semblance of normalcy.

Duncan experienced increasing hopelessness about his life as well. He'd tried counseling and treatment programs. He faithfully attended AA meetings and worked the twelve steps with a sponsor. But he didn't feel better. Finally, one average weekday morning turned into an unforgettable day.

Duncan came downstairs in his stockbroker suit and tie, ready for another eight hours of high-energy appointments and urgent phone calls. He entered the kitchen to say good-bye, his neatly combed hair still wet from the shower. We exchanged a perfunctory kiss on the cheek, and he drove off in his pickup. But less than a mile from home, overwhelming despair forced him to pull over. Later, he explained what happened.

The motor idled, but his thoughts raced. On a hillside with a bird's-eye view of our town, he took account...*my wife, the kids, a brand-new house, nice cars, recreation whenever I want, and plenty of money...why am I so unhappy? I don't drink anymore. The affair is over. So why don't I feel better? I've made such a mess of things with Susan.* He looked out the windshield at the beautiful valley on a spring morning. *I don't even enjoy this. Everything is ruined. What's the use?* As hard as he tried, he couldn't shake the feeling of futility. It was the darkest void he'd ever been in. Now he understood why people shot themselves. In agony he yelled, "God help me! God! Please help me," and stretched out his palms in the cab of his truck, reaching for something unseen.

A calming, powerful presence entered the truck and surrounded him. The presence was magnificent and stunning, yet somehow as real as anything, and even intimate. He knew instantly that it was God. There was no denying it. A serene voice inside his head said, *Everything is going to be okay.* He sensed God telling him that recovery and healing would take time. A perceptible peace flowed over him like soothing water, and his anguish subsided.

Later that day when we met with our counselor at an alcohol treatment program, Duncan felt the same presence come into the room, as intense as it had been before. As the counselor spoke, Duncan wept a stream of tears. I'm not exactly sure what was said, but it was all about Jesus, and in those moments, my husband became a follower of Christ. A heavenly transaction had taken place, and nothing else mattered.

Duncan is a passionate person, and his experience of God was no different. His primordial cry wouldn't have been satisfied with a pastoral platitude. He needed nothing short of an authentic encounter with the God who knew his deepest need. And from that day on, he understood that God was profoundly relational.

From the beginning, he didn't worry about regular church attendance or maintaining a perfect-behavior scorecard. He wasn't compelled to earn a degree in systematic theology. And although helping orphans has become his life's work, he didn't initially run out and start programs for the poor. His initial and lasting expression of faith was a hunger and thirst to know the God who had visited him in his truck. This alone brought deep satisfaction. With guitar in hand, he spent many early mornings singing to his newfound love.

It was just the beginning, but he'd encountered something authentic, and he knew it.

In stark contrast, I grew up in a churched family, but the idea of having a relationship with God was little more than Christian rhetoric. I knew God existed in a general, transcendental sort of way, but I didn't know I was missing something. I wasn't hungry or thirsty for anything. My spiritual experience was all coloring inside the lines.

One day Duncan said, "If you don't have a living, moving, breathing relationship with God, you have nothing." I nodded, agreeing theoretically but wondering, *What does that really mean?* Relationship implied connection, contact. *Sure it had happened to him, but was that possible for me?* Talking to other Christians, I realized my queries were not unique. Everywhere I raised the question, others seemed to share my ignorance. If I mentioned the idea of hearing God's voice or connecting with him in a real way, I'd get the fisheye, or at best, pensive stares. If you actually believe God can speak to people, you risk getting put in the category of crackpots and fanatics. Actual contact sounds far-fetched, ludicrous, and presumptuous. People envision Jim Jones the Kool-Aid leader, David Koresh, and glassy-eyed smiley people.

Nevertheless, as I looked in my Bible, it was hard to miss that God got up close and personal with more than a few people. Moses and

Abraham, for instance. But of course, they were uniquely chosen by God. Maybe I was just a twentieth-century housewife with an overactive imagination. He'd spoken to my husband, but I had been raised in the church and was reluctant to believe in spiritual hocus-pocus. Call it what you will, but I was loyal to the Way-We've-Always-Done-Things type of church.

Then one summer, I decided to study the book of Acts. To my surprise, I found a living, moving, breathing kind of God. The Holy Spirit supernaturally interacted with those first followers as they started building the kingdom of heaven on earth. Something stirred me.

I wanted that. I longed for real contact with God. Living in a different time, under different circumstances, shouldn't exclude me from that sort of relationship. I didn't buy "that was then; this is now." Yet when I looked at all our Christian literature, tapes, sermons, college curricula, and camp programs, the relational aspect of our faith seemed sorely underdeveloped. We give it lip service, telling others our faith is not a religion but a relationship with God, yet we fail to unpack the cliché. True seekers are left hanging. People yearn for a genuine connection with God to the point where they accept substitute gods they can see and touch.

It's nothing new. The Israelites grew tired of waiting for Moses's God and had a golden cow. Lacking the hope of something more tangible and satisfying, are we any different?

If Christianity is a story about restoring *relationship* with God, there must be more to it.

I didn't set out to write a technical how-to manual on experiencing God. Neither is this a theological case for hearing God's voice today. Other authors have ably laid that foundation.[1] I don't pretend to be an authority. These are just some notes I've taken along the way. My hope is that through them you might find something beyond the familiar and the formulaic, and see the possibilities for knowing God yourself.

What you're about to read is how I discovered that God was interacting with me all throughout my life, beginning in my childhood. As I grew up, several obstacles kept me from knowing him. These were gradually overcome. Then I learned to slow down, listen, wait, and notice things that were more than simple coincidence. Hearing God's voice was like learning a new language. I started with the basics and gradually picked up more nuances.

The Bible says, "God speaks once, or twice, *yet* no one notices it." [2] Most people have no template for intimacy with him, yet it isn't enough to simply believe in God. You need more than a religious paradigm. You have to experience him.

I found that God not only spoke in the crises but also in the mundane events of my life. Soon intimacy with God was no longer a myth. He was available, responsive, and interested in making contact. I only had to ask and believe it was possible in the first place. After all, God himself said:

> And you will seek Me and find Me, when you search for Me
> with all your heart. And I will be found by you. [3]

God is knowable.

ONE

Following Alice
Contact with God Is Possible

If you gain, you gain all. If you lose, you lose nothing.
Wager then, without hesitation, that He exists.

—BLAISE PASCAL

n the moment before it happens, a tingling sensation sweeps across your face like a sprinkling of fairy dust. For a few seconds you're not sure if it will come about or just fade away. The person you're with continues to talk, but you can't listen. You don't mean to be rude or anything. It's involuntary, as if you've been pulled out of your life for a moment. You glance toward the sun, because a bright light sometimes brings it on. Almost simultaneously, muscles tighten deep down in your abdomen, surging upward through your chest and shoulders like an unseen, unstoppable force. Your eyes close. They always close. You have no choice in this now. Your body takes over. Your diaphragm heaves and a force rattles your torso, engaging your vocal cords for sound effects.

You have just sneezed.

It's a perfectly normal experience. No one calls 911. It can happen at the most inopportune moments, but the sneezer says nothing more than, "Excuse me." It's happened in every group across cultures, on every continent throughout time. A sneeze is universally understood.

Imagine, if you will, that you had never sneezed in your life. One day you're going about your business when suddenly, a gale force roars up your windpipe. Would you notice it? Of course! You might be ter-rified at first, but over time you'd come to recognize the signals. Whether you were talking, eating, or even driving, you would instinc-tively sense something was imminent. Eventually you could identify a sneeze moment, even if it simply passed by. It's something you would just know in your knowing place. Though mysterious, a sneeze would become a familiar experience.

Years ago, I craved for something like a sneeze to rattle the status quo of my spiritual journey. I knew there was something more than my current experience of God. My church life was okay, but Sunday morn-ing services often left me restless. After years of earnest Bible study, I still searched for something beyond an intellectual assent of faith. Periodi-cally I baptized myself in the bathtub, confessing all my current failures to God. I tried to live out a social gospel—everything from feeding the poor to visiting the elderly. These things were all good, but they were not what I was after.

Something inside me longed for a greater reality. If a relationship with God was really more than just an expression, I wanted to experi-ence it. After all, as author Mike Mason reasoned, we're talking about a God who wasn't satisfied to remain alone in heaven. He wanted to min-gle with us. So he entered the world as a man and joined the common life of his people.[1] Deep inside I felt God had more to give us than church services, Bible knowledge, and programs for the poor. I believed he was actually offering himself.

About the same time, my friend Jenny and I were discussing the idea of hearing God's voice. Now, I'm not talking about an audible voice. That would have been too crazy. And we didn't mean hearing his Word from reading the Bible, as important as that is. I was after some-thing different. I wanted to experience what Jesus meant when he said, "My sheep hear My voice."[2]

That one verse raised so many questions: Is it possible to connect with that kind of a God? Is it presumptuous to think that the Creator of the universe would talk to me? Is he available for a person-to-person exchange like the disciples experienced when Jesus walked shoulder to shoulder with them? I knew that people encountered God in times of crisis. *Guideposts* magazine abounded with examples. But I was looking for a Supreme Being who wanted to interact with me weekly, daily, even moment to moment.

Jenny had wrestled with the same questions years ago. She shared stories of things that had happened to her, situations beyond happenstance. She wondered if God was saying something through these coincidences. I listened with fascination—and concern. I knew presumption could easily sneak in the back door. "How do you know for sure?" I kept asking.

Then one day she told me an analogy that made sense. "You know how it feels when a sneeze is about to happen? You experience a definite sensation. You know something is stirring. It's like that with God."

As a child I believed he was everywhere in a vague sort of way, and I never expected anything more dramatic. But all that changed one summer night in 1976 on a two-lane highway in New Hampshire.

A few years ago I flew from Montana to New Hampshire for a writers conference. After landing at the airport, the Hertz lady handed me a set of car keys and a road map. While studying the directions, a spiritual "sneeze" started to stir. Highway 302, the main road to the conference, took me to a place in my past. *What are the odds that I would return to this particular road in New Hampshire?* Driving north on 302, I experienced a slow-motion déjà vu when entering the town of North Conway. I spent the summer of 1976 in this small New England town.

My college friend Lee-Lee had invited me to stay at her mother's summer cottage there. To pay our way, we hunted for waitressing jobs. During our stay we swam in sparkling waters, lay in the sun, and worked the afternoon and evening shifts at the Scottish Lion, an upscale restaurant and gift shop. After hours, we'd roll up the rugs at the cottage and dance with summer friends to Ella Fitzgerald and Louis Armstrong. One weekend we boarded a ferry to Martha's Vineyard. It was the first time I was really on my own, and life offered many adventures.

I learned to be confident with all kinds of people and soon found that a number of men were forward and some women seemed competitive. I discovered that I had opinions, and people would actually listen. I felt empathy for rejected people in unjust situations. But most of all, I had a desire to write about everything and spent many hours journaling.

And here I was again. My heart flooded with memories as I drove through the familiar scenery of North Conway. Butterfly feelings fluttered through me. *Why did I return? Was it random? Coincidence?*

My questions were soon answered.

Continuing north on Highway 302, I recalled that years ago Lee-Lee and I were on this same stretch of road at 2 a.m. one night in my grandparents' '62 Beetle. As we hummed along the vacant, two-lane road curving rhythmically around the gentle slopes of the White Mountains, a rabbit appeared in front of us, frantically zigzagging. Each time I slowed to give it room, the confused rabbit ran into the grass but returned to the road as soon as I accelerated. Back and forth, this maddening game went on for more than a quarter mile. We followed awhile longer, and finally I pulled over, giving the rabbit an extended chance to get away.

The two-lane highway was narrow and adjacent to a deep ditch, but we managed to edge over onto the sloped ground next to a hillside just before a sharp turn in the road. No sooner had I steered off the road when a semi, passing another car, came barreling around the curve toward us in my lane. The truck roared by inches away, paralyzing us with terror and shaking our little car with hurricane force.

In the silence that followed, my friend and I sat, tilted on the weak shoulder of the empty road, and wept. We didn't speak. But our thoughts were identical. We could have died that night.

How astonishingly fragile life is. A near-head-on collision suddenly framed the immense value of my short time on earth. God had spared our lives by sending a rabbit, and like Alice in Wonderland, I had entered a completely new perception of life. Here in real space and time, the God of heaven intervened in my tangible little world. He could and he did. For some reason, it was not my day to die. The realization was palpable.

Driving along this road again brought the experience back to life. The weight of wonder filled the car, as real in the Hertz rental as it was that night in the Volkswagen Beetle. I had driven to a geographical portal in my life, a place where heaven had penetrated my small place on the earth, and the mystery of a real God enveloped me all over again. Like Old Testament Jews who piled rocks, marking a place where God did something powerful,[3] I had returned in order to remember. God, it seemed, had pulled me out of my routines, my responsibilities, and my driven-every-moment lifestyle to say, "Hey Susan, I'm talking to you." And it came unannounced.

Just like a sneeze.

TWO

Basic Trust
The Father Thing Matters

*(My father) never once told me
he loved me, and he never had
a loving hand to lay on his
children. He said once that he
didn't have to tell people he loved
them for them to know it....
Still, it would have meant an
awful lot for me to have heard it,
just once, before he died.*

—JOHNNY CASH

was only twenty years old that night in New Hampshire on an empty road in a '62 Beetle. Of course, when you're twenty, you know everything. But that night I learned something new, something out of this world, something I sensed down deep but really couldn't prove. I discovered that God was real, he knew who I was, and my earthly life mattered to him. Prior to that remarkable night, I had only fuzzy ideas about God because he was intricately woven into the tapestry of my life. Let me explain.

When I was very young, my family lived on Maplewood Road, a few blocks from Lake Erie. One glorious Indian-summer day, I was playing in the backyard. Red, yellow, and orange leaves fell in great abundance every fall, creating new materials for castle building and fun places to play hide-and-seek.

I remember my father coming down the back-door steps to find me. With great delight, I had hidden myself in the leaves, unaware that my white Keds gave me away. A mixture of fright and glee gripped my three-year-old body: Dad was a zealous tickler. I held my breath as he pretended to search for me. Seconds passed that felt like minutes. My excitement grew unbearable as the sound of crunching leaves came closer…and closer…and then stopped. He took a few more steps. My tiny body grew taut as an inflated balloon. Suddenly, he grabbed my ankle, and I popped up. My piercing squeal turned into peals of giggles for I had been found.

Leaning back, I expected to be tickled, but I looked up to see his kind eyes, his broad smile, and his arm extended toward me. Complete safety exuded from my father's strong and quiet presence. I took his warm hand, and we walked across the yard, the balmy wind swirling leaves around us.

Once inside, we slid into the red vinyl bench that curved around the kitchen table. He took an orange from the bowl on the table. With a paring knife, he sliced off the North and South poles of the peel in little round disks. After cutting the rest of the skin in longitudinal lines, he removed the remaining pieces in sections. I sat riveted, watching his skilled hands maneuver the knife. The pungent scent of orange filled the air, its mist sparkling in the sunlight. At last, he divided the peeled orange into two halves and gave me a section.

As far as I know, until that day I had never tasted an orange. As the sweet juice trickled down my chin, we leaned against each other and laughed in mutual delight. Somehow, this one random moment out of hundreds of thousands in my young life has been crystallized in amber. It is my earliest memory.

Authorities say these early memories, though seemingly arbitrary, are significant. Good or bad, they reveal the perceptions that shape our reality. I fully believe that. Culled from my tender years, this simple snapshot shows how my world was profoundly fashioned by a loving and stable father. I say this because later it took a very small step to believe that *God* is such a father. I know I'm fortunate in this.

When Jesus taught his friends to pray, he gave them a new name for God: "Our Father."[1] Addressing God as a father was a radical departure from Old Testament constructs. The Jews lived with a potent mixture of terror and awe when it came to God, with no such familiarity or warmth. He was called Almighty, the One Who Parted the Red Sea, and Maker of the Cloud by Day and the Pillar of Fire by Night.[2] One could not presume to know him personally.

But Jesus expanded our understanding of God, even referring to him as *Abba*,[3] meaning "Daddy." And through Jesus, God demonstrated his Abba love for us. Like a zealous tickler, he wanted us to experience his strong, knowing touch and our joy at the thrill of this contact. The concept of a heavenly Daddy dovetailed with everything I knew about life. I understood it, because it was already my experience.

Over a hundred years ago, another father lay dying in his bed. Although he was admired as one of Russia's greatest writers, not many knew that Fyodor Dostoevsky was also a great father. Unlike other men of his day, he helped bathe and feed his children. He comforted his little ones at night when he heard coughing or crying. When his daughter Sonya died in infancy, he was inconsolable. To Dostoevsky, children embodied the joy of God.[4]

As his own life was ebbing away, he called for his children. He wanted to read them the story of the prodigal son. As the narrative goes, a son leaves his father and squanders all his inheritance on worthless things. The father grieves the loss but hopes and watches for his son's return. Eventually the son heads home, unsure if he will be welcomed. But when the father sees him coming down the road, he rushes out to meet him, covering him with kisses and assuring him all is forgiven.

When the reading ended, Dostoevsky took their small hands and looked into their tearful eyes.

> My children…never forget what you have just heard. Have
> absolute faith in God and never despair of His pardon. I love
> you dearly, but my love is nothing compared with the love of
> God for all those He has created.… Never despair of God. You
> are His children; humble yourselves…and He will rejoice over
> your repentance.[5]

Later that same night, Fyodor Dostoevsky died, holding his wife's hand.

God is the all-powerful, all-knowing Creator of the universe. But the good news is he is also a *father*. In the final moments of his life, Dostoevsky wanted to impart this sacred knowledge, more than any other truth, to his children. His works are full of the same message, and subsequently, Dostoevsky became a spiritual father to many. Tens of thousands of people followed his funeral procession. Millions more have read his books. But his children heard this truth firsthand from their earthly father, who lived the words he spoke, giving substance to the true nature of God.

Of course, for countless people, this is not the case. Many dads give fathers a poor name. Some children only have bio-dads. Many fatherless souls filter life through cloudy eyes, trying to feel okay, like who cares anyway? But growing up fatherless is not okay. Innumerable people have an invisible dagger lodged deep in their hearts. The wound remains, because their fathers were emotionally unavailable, addicted, abusive, or absent. Abandonment is one of the overriding themes in today's world.

Former professional football player Bill Glass, who worked with inmates in various penitentiaries, said he never met a man in prison who loved his father. Convicts usually made allowances for mothers and occasionally sent Mother's Day cards. But there were no Father's Day cards mailed from the prison. Bill even went so far as to say that fatherlessness may be the root of criminality, because a child without a father starts life feeling cheated already.[6]

In *Blue Like Jazz,* Donald Miller wrote, "I wonder why it is God refers to Himself as 'Father' at all. This, to me, in light of the earthly representation of the role, seems a marketing mistake. Why would God want to call Himself Father when so many fathers abandon their children?"[7] It's a poignant question. Our idea of God is profoundly parallel to whatever happened with our earthly fathers. Miller himself grew up with little contact with his dad. In *To Own a Dragon,*[8] he wrote about the importance of separating his understanding of God from his dad's mistakes. This distinction proves to be significant for many people's spiritual growth.

For me, thinking of God as a loving father made sense. As a child I felt the stirrings of God all around me, but I didn't analyze it as a separate experience. God was warm like the sunlight streaming through the window in winter. He was kind like soft pussy willows on Easter morning. He could also be strict, like when I was told to eat my spinach. But as I rode in the backseat of our Oldsmobile, I never had to worry about where life was going.

One night God reminded me about the pricelessness of a good father through a bedtime story I read to my daughters. We were reading *On the Banks of Plum Creek,* Laura Ingalls Wilder's story about her pioneer family in the 1870s. Pa told his children not to go down to the deep places in the creek without him. But the next day was terribly hot, and Laura decided after much rationalization that she would only go down to the water for a drink. She was trying to remember with all her might what Pa had said. Down the path, she encountered a snarling badger that would not let her pass. Startled, she ran all the way home.

As she lay in bed that night, the thought of disobeying her father gnawed at her. Only the badger knew. But she suffered anyway, knowing she'd dishonored his trust. Finally she slid out of bed and tiptoed to her father who sat just outside the door playing his fiddle under the stars. Out came her tortured confession.

Then for a long time he did not say anything and Laura waited.
Laura could not see his face in the dark, but she leaned against
his knee *and she could feel how strong and kind he was.*[9]

The bedtime reading stopped there. I was undone by the love Laura
felt from her father. I couldn't finish the story. My two daughters, four
and seven at the time, didn't understand my tears, but we silently held
each other while I wept and they wondered.

If I had failed miserably, even in much greater ways than Laura, I
could still lean against my father's knee and feel his strength and his
kindness. Even the prodigal son didn't know if the father would accept
him in his failures. But I knew. Like Laura, I wouldn't have to see my
father's face to know this. And though I can't see God's face, *strength* and
kindness describe his presence to me.

Some will surely say, "Well, that's nice…*for you*…but what am I supposed to do?" We've all had different fathers. It may be harder for fatherless people to understand God's paternal character, but we've all
experienced deficiencies of love. It's not unlike newlyweds who come
from broken homes trying to figure out how to do marriage. It's not
impossible to value love, even without much firsthand experience. Most
of us have some concept of love—a grandfather, a mother, a teacher, a
neighbor. And though God's love is vastly bigger than that, he limits himself so we can approach him without terror. Like a dad holding out an
orange for his child.

Many children are not given unconditional love. Some children are
handed the perfect storm—a crisis on every front. I cannot explain this.
I only know that a big part of intimacy with God involves a basic trust
in his character. When earthly fathers leave us scarred, our view of God
is also damaged. It may feel like an emotional leap to believe God is a
good father.

Even so, God promises to transform our personal history. For many
it will require a step of faith, a willingness to receive a new kind of love

where you won't have to flinch. Though I share Miller's concern for God's alleged marketing mistake, my knowledge of real love keeps me from accepting that limitation.

As I reflect on that fall day when I shared an orange with my dad at the kitchen table, I see a double image of God pulling me into his red-vinyl orbit. He wants to be close and show me something new. I see the earth in his good, strong hands. He unpeels it for me, and it's beautiful, fragrant, and inviting. He wants to do this together. That's the idea here. To experience this life with him and enjoy it while it lasts. One moment soon, it will all be gone. But what remains is the relationship.

There's a Father who's already come out the door of heaven, and he's looking for his child. He knows where to find you. You may think he doesn't know where you are, because you're hiding. But he knows. Maybe you sense him approaching. It seems you've been waiting a long time, wondering if he's coming, hoping he will appear. And then finally, you feel him. He reaches for you, and the moment is thrilling and startling. You won't want to draw back when you look into his face, see his kind eyes and broad smile. His strong arm extends toward you. If you take his hand, something new will begin. Something you've never experienced before.

What I am saying comes down to a simple point: you can know this experience for yourself. Not because I've said so, not because you read it in a book or heard it from a preacher on TV. You can know because this Father understands you and knows where to find you. It can happen.

In fact, you could be anywhere when life with God begins.

THREE

Points of Contact
When Heaven Meets Earth

I make it my business only to persevere in His holy presence...an habitual, silent, and secret conversation of the soul with God, which often causes me joys and raptures inwardly, and sometimes also outwardly, so great that I am forced to use means to moderate them and prevent their appearance to others.

—BROTHER LAWRENCE

From my prerabbit years, I only recall a few sneeze moments when God broke into my consciousness. And it all started with Christmas Eve services when I was a child.

Every Sunday, year in and year out, our church practiced the ritual of hymn singing. Each week the minister of music chose different ones, so I never learned many songs. I spent all my energy trying to sing in the right pitch while glancing at the words and struggling to pull the whole thing together. When I couldn't hit the high notes, I tried harmonizing, but that quickly deteriorated into a sound reminiscent of dog howling. I just didn't get the whole idea of worshiping through hymns.

But Christmas Eves were different. The traditional carols, though hymnlike, were familiar. I knew at least three, maybe even four verses of each song. The whole meaning of worship changed as I sang the songs by and from my heart. Maybe it was the candlelight or the intimacy of the chapel instead of the big sanctuary. Maybe it had to do with all the people packed in the pews—sort of like extended family. You could sit next to someone you didn't know, and it didn't matter if your shoulders touched. In contrast, Sunday mornings seemed formal, polite, and basically uptight.

Something mystical happened to me as a child in a time of true worship. God's presence seemed almost tangible, like a warm breeze in the air. I closed my eyes and sank into the images in the carols: "Yet in thy dark streets shineth the everlasting light."[1] I could feel hope glowing in the candles that shone against the dark. I heard joy in the voices around me and marveled at the sound, as though angels had joined us in harmony. The words felt so otherworldly. Something bright and beautiful had arrived on earth.

Song after song, the lyrics sowed enchanting thoughts into my wide open heart: "Long lay the world, in sin and error pining, till he appeared and the soul felt its worth."[2] Yes, we mattered to God. He had come to rescue us. The kingdom had its King. The theology was beyond my young intellect, but I soaked in the wonder of a Supreme Being who was all about love. I remember after one Christmas Eve service, entering the brisk night air, impervious to the cold. As we drove home, I scanned the sky, looking for the Bethlehem star, trying not to blink.

I think God has an easier time connecting with children because the mental constructs of logical reasoning don't block their receptivity. As an adult, my thinking gets in the way. God says, "For my thoughts are not your thoughts, neither are your ways My ways."[3] I'm not saying that Christians should hang up their brains and go on blind faith. But I have learned that God bypasses my head at times to speak to my heart. My mind tries to organize and pigeonhole God—like trying to analyze a sneeze. But children are wonderfully unencumbered in this way.

Each year on Christmas Eve, my heart longed for God with unfettered emotions. Some might call this true worship. As a child I wasn't intentional about it. I just knew that the warm-blanket feeling of God's presence felt good, and I wanted more of it. But I thought it only happened once a year, like a magic formula. I didn't know connecting with God could be intrinsic to life.

So it was that after decades of hymn singing, one ordinary Sunday I visited a church with contemporary worship. The words and the melodies of this new music were simple, easy to learn, and by the second verse I almost knew the entire song. That morning the church had scheduled a whole hour for music. But after the first few songs, I couldn't sing or even stand with the rest of the people. Tears dropped down my cheeks one after another, creating lines through my makeup. I couldn't stop the flow. A little pile of tissues turned into a big pile. God's presence floated down on me like a dove with soft wings. I desperately needed to connect with the One in charge of the universe. I wanted the embrace of a strong and kind Father—someone who understood my needs. I felt homesick for something I didn't even know I was missing.

I've since realized that experiencing God is not dependent on music and doesn't just occur on Christmas Eve. It doesn't even require a church service. A point of contact can happen anywhere. It's a "sanctuary" I can enter any time, as I study a science book, lie in bed, or take a walk.

Awhile back, I read about a soldier named Nicholas Herman who once found such a sanctuary. Trudging homeward along a snowy trail, he was weary, ready to remove his frozen boots and devour a bowl of hearty soup. Along the way he noticed a mature fruit tree, stripped of its summer beauty. He paused to gaze at the barren tree. In a few short months, leaves would burst forth in vitality. Fireworks of flowers would erupt in radiant colors and fragrance, followed by sweet, luscious fruit, weighing down the branches.

Basking in these thoughts, God's presence descended on him like lacy snowflakes. Time stopped its steady march, and in those sparkling moments, God impressed on his soul an image that was never erased.

Beyond the reality of the barren tree, he saw a "high view of the providence and power of God."[4] I wonder how long he stood there. Later, he told a friend that this single experience produced a love for God in his heart that did not diminish, though forty years had passed.

This young soldier came to be known as Brother Lawrence, a kitchen worker for the Carmelite monks in the 1600s. Like a dormant tree in spring, he awoke from spiritual slumber to realize that God was intimately involved in ordinary life, guiding, renewing, and enjoying. As he worked in the kitchen, he conversed with God while washing dishes and peeling potatoes. Those simple conversations became *The Practice of the Presence of God,* a little book read by millions and still relevant over four hundred years later.

In another century, Albert Schweitzer noticed sunlight streaming through a glass of water. The liquid split the light into a spectrum of colors. Filled with wonder, he was oblivious to everything else in the room. Schweitzer said, "It seemed to me laughable that the wind, the rain, the snow, the hail, the formation of clouds, the spontaneous combustion of hay, the trade-winds, the Gulf Stream, thunder and lightning, should all have found their proper explanation."[5] How could we possibly think we have it all figured out? For Schweitzer, acknowledging God in the mystery was a point of contact.

For others, scientific study is a catalyst for connecting with God, as my friend Vanessa discovered while on a date with her soon-to-be husband, Kyle. As an eye doctor, Kyle had studied the science of vision for years in medical school, but he never got over the marvel of it. He described to his fiancée how our vision system processes more information in a minute than the most powerful computers in the world can process in a day. The optic nerve alone has over a million nerve fibers coming from all over the eye's retina. He told her how the cornea is the fastest healing tissue in the entire body, able to heal in a day. The more he learned in medical school, the more he wondered how anyone could think there wasn't a Creator.

But some spiritual moments are not warm and inspiring. Sometimes contact with God is discomforting. Perhaps the most interesting part of Philip Yancey's book *Disappointment with God* comes at the very end when Yancey describes what he called his first authentic religious experience. At college in the middle of a prayer group that felt obligatory, he decided to pray out loud. Ordinarily silent, Yancey secretly entertained agnosticism, but that day he spilled his frustration with God. With brutal honesty, he admitted that he didn't want to reach other students for Christ. In fact, he couldn't care less.

Suddenly, Yancey had a vision of himself as the wounded victim in the Good Samaritan story. As he looked up from the ditch, the kind Samaritan took on the face of Christ. Jesus approached him and tried to clean his wounds, but Yancey spit at him full in the face. It all happened in slow motion. Abruptly he stopped praying, got up, and left the room, but the experience impacted the rest of his life.[6]

Like Yancey, I was sorting out many spiritual questions in my college years. I had an ongoing argument with God about why he would risk it all by giving man a free will. I was acutely aware of unjust suffering in the world. Life was an experiment gone awry—profoundly awry. If you can believe it, I remember weeping at a fraternity party to the bewilderment of my boyfriend. My generation seemed lost and confused, destroying their lives with drugs, alcohol, and random sex. But you see, I was ruled by my intellect then. My mind was angry at God, but my spirit longed for him.

During those years, I tried going to church but felt overwhelmingly restless. The children's choir sang something to the effect of "I'm so happy, happy, happy—in Jesus all the time." But I watched the clock, waiting for the last hymn and benediction. Christianity didn't seem relevant to the suffering world outside, and I didn't know how to reconcile the mixed message for myself, much less for others.

Yet soon, the love of God began to woo me through stories. I found solace in the novels of Dostoevsky. At the time he was my favorite author.

He didn't ignore the groaning of creation. Instead he brought God squarely into the middle of it all.

The Brothers Karamazov is considered by some to be Dostoevsky's masterpiece. Sigmund Freud wrote that *The Brothers Karamazov* is "the most magnificent novel ever written, and the story of the Grand Inquisitor is one of the peaks in the literature of the world. It can hardly be overpraised."[7] But I wasn't reading the story for its literary value. The text was rich with spiritual questions and observations, yet I wasn't looking for theological answers either. Strange as it may seem, I found comfort for my questioning heart. Though his masterpiece is fiction, it felt alive with faith.

Dostoevsky was spiritually genuine. He had passed through the long dark tunnel of atheism. He wrote, "My hosanna has come forth from the crucible of doubt."[8] Something vital and utterly life giving oozed out of his pores and spilled into everything he wrote. My spiritual awareness was heightened as I read along, desperately grasping at the hope that God was real and could be known here on earth, here in our human condition.

The Brothers Karamazov is a story of patricide. Dostoevsky put a piece of himself in each of the four brothers. Alyosha is the childlike Christian, Dmitri is the hedonist, Ivan portrays an intellectual cynic, and Smerdyakov is the rejected illegitimate brother. Although Smerdyakov murders his father, three of the four are guilty by hatred. Only Alyosha has clean hands.

"The Grand Inquisitor" is the section in which Ivan tells Alyosha an allegory about Jesus and the church that sums up his rejection of Christianity. In Ivan's story, Jesus returns to the earth, but not in all the glory of the Second Coming. Instead, he comes as before—a man among men.

The setting of Ivan's fictitious story is sixteenth-century Spain during the horrors of the Inquisition. The church is steeped in burning heretics at the stake. During this tragic stage of human history, Jesus enters the scene, humbly walking through the surging masses.

People are drawn to him by an invincible force, they flock to him, surround him, follow him. He passes silently among them with a quiet smile of infinite compassion. The sun of love shines in his heart, rays of Light, Enlightenment, and Power stream from his eyes and, pouring over the people, shake their hearts with responding love. He stretches forth his hands to them, blesses them, and from the touch of him, even only of his garments, comes a healing power.[9]

In Ivan's story, the head of the church is the Grand Inquisitor, and he stops after seeing the crowd so aroused. His face grows dark as he witnesses the miracles from a distance. Pointing to Jesus, he tells his guards to arrest him and throw him in prison. When night falls, the heavy door creaks open and the Grand Inquisitor enters to speak his mind. He says Jesus chose poorly in the wilderness of temptation, and that Satan understood the solution for mankind. People can't handle the freedom God offers. Freedom to choose between good and evil has all but destroyed the world and made humanity utterly lost. The world will follow anyone who gives them bread and demonstrates their power to control. If Jesus had bowed to Satan, he could have saved the whole world instead of only a select few. He tells Jesus the human race no longer needs him, and his presence is interfering with the purposes of the church. Jesus never says a word. In the end, he kisses the Grand Inquisitor and departs.

At first, I agreed with Ivan. But a part of me loved Jesus more. I laid the book on my lap, intensely conscious of the opposing points of view swirling in my heart and mind. Yet the picture of Jesus in the midst of that crowd—loving, touching, and healing—outshined the confrontation in the jail cell. God risked the enormous downside of human free will to make way for a kingdom of freedom and hope.

I don't know how, but I attended "church" that day through the power of story. I worshiped at the thought of Jesus walking among us again. I opened my heart to a heavenly Father who rejected compromise, power trips, domination of carnal kingdoms, and instead gave people the freedom to choose his love or not.

God came looking for me that day as I read in my dorm room. He wanted to be found. He came without notice, in an unplanned situation, through a seemingly random chapter in a huge novel. Yet, I believe from his perspective, the moment was entirely intentional. He was only waiting for my heart to engage.

God is all about these points of contact. He's not playing hide-and-seek. It's much more serious than that. Jesus called it "seek, and…find."[10] And as far as I know, for anyone who's willing, the invitation still stands.

FOUR

Love Came Down
God Doesn't Want to Date Forever

The gospel to me is simply irresistible.

—BLAISE PASCAL

D ag Hammarskjöld in his book *Markings* wrote, "Without the strength of personal commitment, your experience of others is at most aesthetic."[1] It's like observing a beautiful painting but never feeling the stroke of a brush in your hand or smelling the pungent odor of oil paint when you open a tube. It's far more engaging to blend shades of calm greens, deep blues, or luscious reds on a palate, creating shapes, shadows, and movements on what was merely a blank white canvas.

Whenever I choose to get involved with something—a painting, a new job, a relationship—I stop being a spectator and enter the fray. I deny my self-preservation instinct and open my life to dynamic possibilities.

Because engaging with God is so vitally important, he brings us to a decision of commitment, a point where we either break up or give it all. He offers us a real interpersonal encounter. He knows we're all too content to be religious, rub elbows with him, and never get very serious. But he is passionate and isn't willing to take no for an answer. He pursues and woos, and ultimately he proposes.

I will tell you how it happened to me.

In November 1968, I officially entered teenhood. Already immersed in the hypersophisticated culture of junior high, I had a certain awareness of what was cool and what was not. At the time, popularity depended on things like pointed shoes with buckles and white lipstick. My dad, seeing my white lips, asked if I was cold. I didn't think it was funny. At school I received a surfer's cross from a boy named Matt who wanted to "go out" with me. My mother said, "And *where,* exactly, will you be going?" My parents just didn't understand how important these developments were in a young girl's life. After Matt and I became an item, I felt sure I was on the verge of saying hi to the popular girls in choir.

Like most teenage girls, a large part of my identity was focused on gaining acceptance from my peers. Basically that meant an overemphasis on clothes. Of course, the style changed about every week, depending on what Nancy and Francey wore. The only thing that didn't change was the straight hair, parted-down-the-middle style of the sixties. So clothes became our unique statement. If I was going to make an impression, I had to keep up. I was too young for a real job and my monthly allowance wasn't enough.

Essentially, it all came down to a little shoplifting.

Around this time, something inside me became strangely curious to learn what it felt like to be bad. As a naturally compliant child, I received life as it was handed to me. Things had gone pretty well. But being good all the time had become a little boring, like life without cosmetics. In short, shoplifting was more than a financial necessity—it was a subtle form of questioning everything I had been taught.

Realizing I actually thought this way feels a bit like looking off a high ledge with no railing. But crossing moral boundaries is a standard scenario for teens. And of course, rebellious experimentation has reached far scarier proportions, oral sex being the latest junior high party favor. My choice to shoplift seems somewhat benign in retrospect. But in my world at the time, it was no less daring.

In God's view, stealing stuff served a vital purpose: to drive home the reality of sin. You see, I was such a good kid that it was hard to believe God on the subject. The Bible says God's kindness leads someone to repentance, but how could that happen if someone didn't think they'd sinned in the first place? Like many people, I figured I was okay with God because I wasn't a serious criminal. I'd take my chances at heaven's door that God would be a kind old grandfather and overlook the minor details. After all, Santa gave us gobs of presents even when we were a little bit naughty.

Now I understand why God takes each of us away from the mirage of our own goodness and out to the edge of free will. There, we can get a good look at the abyss of sin. He has to show us what we are apart from him, because important choices are made there, and it's a crucial step in the process of finding God. Otherwise, Christianity could be relegated to just an interesting idea with little application.

As a young teen, I had only a vague concept of sin. I didn't speak Christianese. Theological phrases like "redeemed by the blood" or "propitiation for sin" made no sense to me. God was in his heaven, and I was just a young girl keeping up with the popular girls in choir. I didn't know that I needed a special connection with God, and that sin blocked the relationship.

But secretly sliding a pair of new sunglasses into my coat pocket at the department store showed me something new about myself. Sin was real. Inside I knew right from wrong, but I didn't want to stop. The thrill of getting something for nothing felt powerful. By fourteen, I had become skilled in petty theft. Yet all along, God was setting the stage for what would happen the following summer when I went abroad.

My paternal grandparents wanted all their grandchildren to experience Europe. Though my grandfather didn't live long enough to see this vision through, my grandmother was determined to fulfill their plan. The summer of 1970, my sister, Nancy, our cousin Patti, and I left for a three-week, eight-country tour of Europe with our Gram. The grandsons would go on trips later.

We took in amazing sites—Westminster Abbey, the Crown Jewels, the Eiffel Tower, the Swiss Alps, St. Mark's Square, the Vatican, and the Sistine Chapel—to mention a few. Of course, as teenage girls we were more interested in sitting in the back of the bus, making signs that read "Ciao, Baby" to hold up when a car of cute boys drove by. We sang our favorite songs by The Temptations, like "Psychedelic Shack" and "Cloud Nine," coordinating our dance movements to the music. And when the bus stopped at gift shops and stores, I continued to steal.

But our favorite amusement soon became making fun of a geeky-looking boy on our bus. We nicknamed him Fergus, so we could talk about him in secret. He wore high-top, black-and-white Converse All Star tennis shoes, and whenever he stood still, his feet would assume the same odd position: heels together with toes pointing out. First position, in ballet terms. Not so good for a teenage boy.

For some reason, we obsessed on this. His feet were hilarious. We wrote him mean anonymous notes and took pictures of his feet. I had joined a pack mentality, and I feel a certain shame now as I write. Yet again, God was clarifying the issue of sin.

Soon something unplanned happened. Our travel group was offered tickets to the Oberammergau Passion Play. Apparently this was highly unusual. The play was performed only during the first year of a new decade, and tickets were always sold out years in advance. In short, we were given a rare opportunity.

The play is a world-famous presentation of the life, death, and resurrection of Jesus Christ. The tradition started in Oberammergau, Germany, in 1634, following an outbreak of the bubonic plague in Europe. The plague had already killed 15,000 people in nearby Munich. The terrified inhabitants of Oberammergau gathered and prayed for God's protection, pledging as a community to do something to honor God forever if he rescued them from the Black Death. The plague swept through Europe killing millions of people, but Oberammergau, Germany, was completely spared. As a result, the townspeople vowed to present the story of Christ to the world every ten years, and they've kept their promise for centuries.

The play involves more than 2,000 Oberammergauers, as actors, singers, instrumentalists, and stage technicians. Men start growing out their hair and beards a year in advance to be consistent with the time period of Jesus's day. The play is performed on an open stage, incorporating the natural scenery into the backdrop, and the auditorium seats almost five thousand people.[2]

The play was an all-day affair performed entirely in German, which could have been extremely boring to three hyperactive teen girls. But when the choir sang, the sound of hundreds of voices in unison captured our restless attention. We were completely entranced. Suffice it to say, there were no Fergus pictures that day.

The crucifixion involved several hundred people on the enormous stage. The depiction was an authentic mob scene with people shouting, pushing, and fighting to attack Jesus. When they arrived at Golgotha, as though on cue, the sky began to fill with dark ominous clouds. Soon a thunderstorm sent lightning crashing in all directions behind the open-air stage. But the play continued undeterred, people wailing and falling, tears mixing with the dust on their wet faces. I was captivated, barely breathing. Nancy wept, holding her head in her hands at times, and Patti seemed paralyzed. Gram's cheeks were wet with tears. I was transported back to that moment in history, centuries from my real life, to a place I'd only heard of in two-dimensional stories from the Bible.

Suddenly this play was bigger than Sunday school and church potlucks. Jesus wasn't just some handsome, Caucasian guy holding a baby sheep. He wasn't American either. God was intimately acquainted with these people in Oberammergau, Germany. He knew their ancestors and their story, and they knew his. Moved by their unabashed faith, he answered their desperate prayers hundreds of years ago. And here, generations later, was a people true to their word, a faithful community presenting Christ in magnificent pageantry, an unmatched spectacle in the world of theater. And God had joined in with the wind, thunderbolts, and darkened sky.

There in my seat, something deep inside me shifted. Something significant, maybe even supernatural, had taken place. And it was all about this man, Jesus Christ.

But this was only the first part of what happened that summer.

Our three weeks in Europe ended, and we returned home. Shortly after, according to God's design, my sister left for a Young Life camp in Colorado, an alternative youth group for churched and unchurched high schoolers. When she returned, I asked her what had happened at camp.

By then, we were at our cabin on the French River in Ontario for the last few golden weeks of summer. Our family had taken a picnic lunch to a white-water area, and Nancy and I had climbed out on a granite ledge. We had played there many summers as children with our miniature birch-bark canoes and tiny dolls. Little waterfalls trickled through spaces in the massive stones, each rock intimately familiar.

Nancy told me that something had changed. She wasn't the same person after her week at Young Life camp. She was barely sixteen years old, yet as my sister spoke about God, she seemed like a wise old seer. I don't remember exactly what she said, but she used phrases like "a personal God," "a relationship with Christ," and "making a decision to believe."

And as I pondered these things, love came down and surrounded me like soft sunlight shining through the leaves. In some uncanny way, God was there. My skin tingled from head to toe as if an angel had tapped my shoulder, Tinker Bell fashion. I looked up fully expecting to see something. Everything around me shifted into slow motion. Even the roar of the white water behind us grew distant.

My sister was still talking, but I only saw her lips moving. I had slipped into a world of my own thoughts. And from deep inside, the word *yes* bubbled to the surface. *Yes. I believe this.* Spoken silently in my heart but heard by God.

My shoplifting days ended in that moment. Suddenly being popular and stealing new clothes lost all its appeal. I didn't like the person I had become in junior high. I wanted to know God and live in his ways.

For some reason tucked away in the mind of God, I was never caught during my shoplifting forays. I shudder now at the prospect of what could have happened, especially for my grandmother in a foreign country. But God is not random in the way things take place. It seems his purposes were served.

In his passion to enter the low lintel of the human heart, God's efforts are incredibly diverse. Some think we are out to find God. Yet, he pursued me to the point of commitment. He knew my address. He had a plan, perfectly tailored to my persona. He revealed the nature of sin, not as a concept but as something evident in my life. He arranged for unexpected tickets to a historic play and even participated in the last scene. With perfect choreography and timing, my sister came home with a clear message I had somehow missed during all those years in church. Heavenly love floated down with the sunlight and encircled me, reaching my innermost being. And I believed in God in a childlike way. My spiritual understanding was limited, yet God was pleased. He had much more to show me before I would fully appreciate the commitment I made that summer day.

Commitment seems like a stuffy old idea in a trendy, fast-paced, non-committal world. Yet for me, it symbolized the beginning of an adventure: to find the substance of God's glory. Author Mike Mason describes commitment as something that takes us to the "deep and unknown waters. For that is its very purpose: to get us out beyond our depth, out of the shallows of our own secure egocentricity and into the dangerous and unpredictable depths of a real interpersonal encounter." [3]

God offers that real interpersonal encounter, a heaven-on-earth connection with himself. And when we choose to cross that threshold, out of aesthetic experience and into personal commitment, life will never be the same.

FIVE

Got Religion?
The Obstacle of Religiosity

We are in an age of religious complexity. The simplicity which is in Christ is rarely found among us. In its stead are programs, methods, organizations, and a world of nervous activities which occupy time and attention but can never satisfy the longing of the heart.

—A. W. TOZER

On a granite ledge by a beautiful river one lazy afternoon in August, I entered the kingdom of God. We went home to the same church. I had the same friends and the same hairstyle. But inside, the shift had already taken over my heart. As Tolstoy said, "True life is lived when tiny changes occur." [1]

In the days of my fledgling faith, I saw everything with new eyes. I lived in the sweet, sunny spot of grace, a land flowing with milk and honey. When I opened my Bible, the text seemed rich with discovery, full of poetry and profound sayings. I scribbled my favorite verses in a notebook.

That fall, Young Life leaders started a club in our area. It was the beginning of the seventies, and the Jesus Movement was well underway. God was breaking out of the religious box all over, and Young Life was on the scene. Jesus entered the popular culture, swiftly dismantling religious archetypes of "church-ianity." Norman Greenbaum's song "Spirit in the Sky" was named song of the year by *Cashbox Magazine*.[2] Soon after, the Doobie Brothers wrote "Jesus Is Just Alright," and everyone I knew was singing along.

Young Life rented a white community house in Bay Village near the lake. The Tuesday night meetings were the high point of my week. We called it "club," and sometimes as many as two hundred kids flocked to the gathering, because, well, it was fun.

A typical club night included songs, funny skits, and a short talk. Leaders read the New Testament narrative in everyday jargon, and the scenes came to life. For example, "Jesus hung out at the Nazareth Community College but decided he would find his first followers down at the Galilee Marina. He was looking for fishermen." The characters became people in our world, people we might have known. They jarred my preconceived ideas about the Bible.

Jesus was compelling. No one rolled their eyes. Girls stopped flirting with boys. I was spellbound, hanging on every word as if I'd never heard anything so interesting in church. If God had bothered to send Jesus to earth, he had to be personal, relational. Better yet, if Jesus *was* God in the flesh, think of the ramifications. God came in our skin, walking in sandals and wearing clothes just like us. My mind soared with the thought.

My childhood paradigm of God was so different. God was pleasant, but kind of serious. He wanted me to be good, act nice, and sit still in church. These unspoken expectations ruled Sunday morning behavior. If pictures of God existed, surely he would look something like Abraham Lincoln—kind, but not exactly cheery. Of course, God had good reasons to be solemn, because he cared about starving children in India. He knew about the mafia in Chicago and witch doctors in Africa. With problems all over the world, how could he smile? God had a lot to worry about, so I couldn't bother him with my little concerns or talk to him in a casual way. Our family prayers were short and reserved. I believed God was gracious and good, but not personal or familiar. I couldn't—wouldn't—imagine God wearing sandals.

Too often, false beliefs about God are absorbed through our experiences of the people who represent him. I mixed God and church people into the same stereotype. If we don't *know* God, we don't have much else to go on. Even though my parents demonstrated God's unconditional love, many of my perceptions about him were also shaped by Sunday morning formalities. I thought Christians were unexciting, insipid people. I couldn't picture them at a party. On Sundays, fun happened after church when we stopped at McDonald's or read the comics section of the paper. Fun was what we did in normal life when God left on a business trip. I learned through Young Life that Christians could be fun, vibrant, and happy. Young Life Christians helped erase my concept of a God who didn't smile.

My mom's cousins Sue and Mary had both married Young Life leaders, Rick and Cliff respectively. Their families have a cabin called Juniper Hill just down the shoreline from our cabin. When our vacation times overlapped, there was no telling what would happen day to day.

One ungodly early morning, the Juniper Hill crew trekked through the woods like a marching band with makeshift instruments consisting of anything from the kitchen with noise-making potential. The band was a replay of the "New Ashmolian Marching Society of the Students Conservatory Band" that regularly performed at the summer camps in the typical zany humor of Young Life. The whole bay could hear them coming through the woods on the trail that connected our cabins. I dove under the covers with a big grin on my face, knowing they had come to wake us up. The door burst open, and Rick, the bandleader, announced the new day's arrival. Soon they dragged my sister and me out to the patio for jumping jacks and toe touches. Clad in our pajamas, barefooted, and bed-headed, we only pretended to be annoyed.

Early morning calisthenics were just one way the Juniper Hill families brought God and fun into the same equation. I remember costume parties, fish fries, water-skiing off the dock, swimming in the moonlight, fishing trips, and blueberry-pancake breakfasts. They always had stashes of candy bars and maple leaf cookies at their cabin that they freely offered—between meals, no less. This radically redefined all the rules about sugar, which was a controlled substance in my family. But all the fun and laughter didn't depend on sugar. Their faith was as unrestrained as their exuberance for life.

On Sundays, when we had church together at one of our cabins, their love for God was evident, but it didn't end with the service. Discussing spiritual things came naturally to them. Their relationship with God spilled over into everyday conversation as they set the table or fried the walleye. They talked about Jesus as if he lived in the neighborhood or might even stop by for dinner. All of this intrigued me, for I had only known a staid, religious sort of Christ.

But over the next few years, my faith inevitably changed when faced with the challenge of "living it out." It didn't happen overnight, but I noticed it in the latter years of high school. My faith had morphed into a religion of duty and obligation. I began straddling the fence between what the Bible said and what the world offered. I experienced the force of temptation, the misery of failure, and the sting of ridicule. Sunday mornings came, and I didn't really want to go to church. It was just a show; my heart was disconnected. I didn't sign up with Jesus to go through rituals and routines. I wanted peace, joy, and love and even believed I could know God. So what happened?

Someone once said, "If you're a Christian, would you please notify your face?" Very funny, but at the time, the thought made me uncomfortable. Why had I become so glum?

For many, including me, the experience of faith gradually diminished into a lifeless form of religion—a set of rules, a list of duties, and all the tension of still being human. Some people did the church thing like clockwork. Numerous others read the Bible, gave money, and served the poor. Other new believers quit using drugs or stopped living with a boyfriend, and some gave up smoking and swearing. All that was good, but it didn't mean beans if we weren't cultivating something more real with God. Without relationship, the Christian experience was gutted.

Perhaps you can relate.

I woke up one day feeling as though being a Christian only added a plethora of new things to my to-do list. Aside from the usual responsibilities, there were fellowship groups, committee meetings, food drives, fund-raisers, book studies, church camps, and vacation Bible school. Even now, I feel a wave of utter exhaustion just typing the words *vacation Bible school.* Or how about my not-to-do list, the lifestyle changes I made to avoid any lingering guilt? I wondered if God was disappointed with me, because I wasn't living up to some indefinable standard of a good Christian life. God required more than I bargained for, and most of it was in the fine print.

I felt trapped.

Religiosity was the counterfeit of all I had hoped for, like owning a state-of-the-art kitchen, studying recipe books, and cooking fantastic meals—but never eating. The people in its grip are starving to death and don't know why. It's going through the motions, the trappings, and the appearance of faith, but missing the substance of it.[3]

Religion is a major pitfall for countless Christians, and it doesn't seem to matter if you are a brand-new Christian or have been around the church for decades. It's the same trap regardless of age, sex, race, or denomination. Many people stuck in religious activities and endless programs think this defines their faith. They may know all about God biblically but can't say they actually *know* him.

Maybe they don't believe it's possible.

Young Life leaders tried to help me along, but I felt stuck in a squirrel cage of obligation. The time I spent with God was highly regimented. I even had a checklist. First, I designated at least five minutes to thank God for whatever came to mind. Then I read something from the Old Testament, followed by something in the New. Sometimes I memorized a favorite verse. To finish, I prayed for others for at least ten minutes. Eventually I knew so many people, I had to divide my list over different days of the week. When rushed for time, I would say a general prayer for "everybody on my Tuesday list" believing that God knew the gist of their needs. I was so systematic in my endeavor to be a good Christian, I didn't leave any room for God to say or do anything. My time with him became something I had to accomplish, instead of a point of contact.

I heard once that missionaries in Africa were concerned about native women who carried heavy burdens on their heads for long distances. The missionaries decided to fix the problem by giving the women small aluminum wheelbarrows. After a time, the missionaries returned to see how the women were doing and found them carrying the wheelbarrows on their heads! Religion without relationship is like that. It just adds one more burden to the load.

For all my religious activities, I fell far short of relationship. I didn't know God; I didn't even know how to know him. I thought faith consisted of everything I had to do for him. Like busy bees around a hive, many Christians keep churning out programs to make sure the agenda is complete, but Jesus is on the outside, knocking to come in. He said this to his followers in Revelation and called them back to relationship, beyond the buzz of activity.[4]

Part of the problem was that I didn't expect God to do anything. I prayed but didn't look for any answers. I figured God had already done his part. He created me, loved me, and forgave me. The rest was up to me. If I succeeded at carrying out my religious patterns, I was a "good Christian." But this led to self-reliance and pride. On the other hand, if I failed, I'd end up in a quagmire of guilt and a far-away-from-God routine. Both outcomes sabotaged any communion with God.

The Christian life seemed like a lose-lose proposition.

During my high school years, this spiritual roller coaster created an internal tension that never existed in my childhood. Religion became something I had to keep whipped up all the time. My new understanding of God through Jesus had been beautiful. I sought him in earnest, but then my fervor ebbed away. When I left for college, I had all but lost my new-convert enthusiasm. Weary of Bible study, I prayed prayers that seemed flat and lifeless. Was this whole Christian thing a mirage? Was I fooling myself? Perplexed and worn out, my faith entered a time of complacency. Furthermore, my lifestyle eventually became compromised. I didn't walk away from my faith, but I certainly drifted.

During this season, God spoke to the inner struggle of my soul. One night, he gave me a dream using clear images, symbolic to my life.

In the dream, I'm driving a half-sunk car to a half-sunk sailboat in the middle of a wide river. Jumping into the boat, I find a gallon-sized Clorox container with the bottom cut off. I use it to bail out the excess water down by my ankles. Before long, I notice the boat is drifting downstream. The river's current seems to be getting stronger by the minute with the vigor of tidal power. I scramble to the front of the boat, looking for a paddle. Inside the hull, I find a dinged-up old oar. It would have to do. I paddle with all my might, stopping only to bail the bilge water churning at my feet.

The current is incredibly forceful. Frantically, I steer the boat to the nearest shore with my foot on the tiller. It takes all my strength to keep the boat heading toward land. The tidal current swirls the bow to the left, then sharply to the right. Back and forth I paddle and bail but make little headway. Looking downstream, I have the distinct impression a waterfall is just around the bend.

Suddenly, I awoke and let out a gasp.

As I lay in bed wondering about the dream, I realized it was an allegory of my struggle with religiosity. The river was the journey of my life. The half-sunk car represented my human existence without God. The car didn't work very well in a river and depended on a limited source of power. The half-sunk sailboat represented my potential life with Christ, a whole new God-powered way to travel on earth. Because I had a sin nature, there was some bailing to do. The tidal current could have represented many different things: personal struggles, the power of the culture, or even spiritual warfare. Somehow I had to get through it all in my own strength.

Then a question floated to the surface of my mind: why didn't I put up the sail? It flat out never occurred to me. I had sailed in real life on Puget Sound and experienced the wind's power over the tidal current. Yet in the dream, I never once thought of the sail.

The metaphor was strong. I thought that getting out of that situation depended on paddling and bailing. The entire focus of the dream centered on my effort, my human striving to get through life. But the sail would have solved everything, and I missed the point entirely. God had designed my life to receive unlimited power to move forward, out of danger, against the current, and safely to shore. Instead I was tossed and turned by the tide.

The danger of religiosity comes when we fail to hoist the sail. We never get in a posture to receive what God will give us to navigate this life and overpower the raging currents. We develop programs, sit on committees, and attend church, filling our time with religious activities. We try to be good people, or at least keep up the appearance. Frankly, it's exhausting, and sadly, that's the best-case scenario.

Because you see, religiosity also has a dark side; the Pharisees were the prototype. Today we have ministers who manipulate their flocks for more money. Some believers are told they will go to hell if they attend the wrong denomination. Others perform certain rituals to pay for their sins. Religiosity is the pointing finger, the whispering tongue, the haughty eye. There is a pride of faith that says, "I am more spiritual than you" or "our church is really something, because we have a new building." It's the reason many people think Christians are lemon-sucking legalists and hatemongers. But most of all, religiosity is the worst form of pride and, therefore, a major strategy of the enemy, entrapping people of faith since the beginning of time.

Unfortunately, an element of religiosity exists in every church, and if you're honest, you will know that no one is immune. I have seen this dark corner in my own heart and feel compelled to deal with its first appearance.

But here's the deal. God never asked us to live the Christian life in our own strength. If he had, we might as well be practicing atheists. Ultimately, religiosity is destructive, because it obscures the fact that God is reaching out to us in love. The wind may blow all around us, but with no effect. We may stand taller than the pack, but miss the joyride of a lifetime.

We have to put up the sail and catch the wind.

As far as I know, there's only one cure for religiosity and that is a relationship with God. To know him is all important. Everything else is just paddling and bailing.

SIX

Never Good Enough
The Trap of Condemnation

*Guilt is the source of
sorrows, the avenging fiend
that follows us behind with
whips and stings.*

—NICOLAS ROWE

A few lanky teens played Hacky Sack by the church entrance as people streamed toward the doors from all directions. Parking spots were getting harder to find. A cross section of our town showed up for the evening—a university professor, a mother with small children, a pair of teenage girls wearing one-size-too-small clothing, a school janitor, a man with a ponytail who worked at the ski hill—to mention a few. Though diverse, all were ordinary, small-town people, and I was one of them.

We settled into our seats as the visiting pastor tested his microphone. A small girl wiggled down the row toward her mother who promptly handed her some crayons and paper to keep her occupied. The speaker began with three questions.

"How many of you think God is love?" A multitude of hands rose like a stirred flock of birds and then gradually settled into their respective laps. The answer was obvious.

"Okay, how many of you think God loves you personally?" he asked. I lifted my hand, but noted fewer hands in the air this time. Why such easy Sunday-school-type questions? The speaker scanned the room and smiled faintly, allowing an extended pause before asking the third question.

"Now then, how many of you *experience* God's love in a tangible way on a regular basis?" I noticed only a few hands in a room of several hundred people. The discrepancy was striking, and perplexing.

For countless people, a mysterious gap exists: we believe in God's love, but we aren't experiencing it firsthand. There may be numerous reasons for this contradiction between desire and reality, yet the most likely cause is the lie of *condemnation.* Also known as *guilt* and *shame,* condemnation is a pervasive barrier keeping countless people from intimacy with God.

Condemnation forms when people believe God is disappointed with them. They wonder if their mistakes have tipped God's scale from favor to scorn. Their failings range from skipping church to visiting porn sites or any number of self-imposed standards of goodness. Many sincere but struggling people live under the gray cloud of their shortcomings. Guilt blocks the light of heavenly love, and eventually the warmth of God's affection feels far away and even nonexistent.

For some, it goes beyond feeling ashamed of bad choices to a core belief that they themselves are bad. This is called shame, and its effect is usually far more destructive. In time, those trapped by shame speculate that God is not merely indifferent, but actually against them. They feel hopelessly flawed and irredeemable. Tragically, these beliefs are rarely spoken out loud, and therein lies their power.

Everywhere I go, I see the shadow of condemnation on people's faces. My friend Ted prays formal set prayers and is never quite sure he's saved. He has gone forward to "receive Christ" many times in church. Stuck at the entrance of his faith, he does not grow beyond a basic knowledge of God.

Then there's Cindy, who believes she is outside God's forgiveness after several abortions. She goes to church regularly but never feels close to him. When she reads Scripture, especially the Old Testament, it reinforces her perception of a judgmental God. Her standing before him is sketchy at best.

Michael grew up in a religious family with high standards. His parents seemed like perfect people, but he has an ongoing struggle with lust. Even now, no matter how hard he tries, perverse fantasies about women still enter his thoughts. He manages to keep up a "Hey, things are great" exterior, but he feels ashamed before God.

Josie, the oldest child in an abusive, alcoholic home, assumed many adult responsibilities growing up. She believed if she was good enough, her parents would stop drinking. Now she apologizes for everything, even when it's not her fault. She always gives up something for Lent to secure favor with God, and she's one of the few people at church who volunteer constantly.

Condemnation doesn't look the same in each of these lives, but the underlying belief is similar: *God is disappointed in me.*

Condemnation themes overshadowed my own young faith, because I lived under an unspoken and mistaken idea. I believed God forgave all my past mistakes, but as an adult Christian, I knew better. Scripture, I thought, supported this belief. When Jesus rescued the woman caught in adultery, he didn't condemn her; however, he said, "From now on *sin no more.*"[1] His words were chilling, but I accepted the mandate. Apparently, God's favor depended on my ability to live a sinless life. If I wanted to know a perfect God, my post-conversion failures created a constant dilemma. Condemnation drizzled grayness over my life, wrecking the picnic and the parade, and ultimately, kept me at a spiritual standstill.

Ironically, in my pre-Christ life I assumed I was good enough for God and his heaven, because I wasn't a hardened criminal. Later as a believer, I rarely felt good enough, sweating over hairsplitting details of Good Christian Behavior.

Not everyone responds to condemnation the same. Some choose to lead a double life. Others coexist with the tension. Some get depressed. A number of people stop going to church. A few become hyperspiritual, and still others punish themselves with some form of penance. In my life, appeasing God with good works became my modus operandi.

But how much and how often? Enough was never enough. No matter how I tried, I still lived under a vague feeling of God's dissatisfaction. I'd spend a Saturday working with elderly people in inner-city Cleveland, but on Sunday I was a surly teenager with my mom. Or I'd lead a discussion group on the topic of sexual purity at church, but still cut my bathing suit to show more cleavage at the pool. Surely God felt exasperated with me, like Moses was when he found the Israelites worshiping a golden calf. I pictured God with crossed arms, saying, "Haven't you got it together yet?"

You'd think I'd be drawn to other verses in the Bible, like Romans 8:1 where Paul explicitly said, "Therefore there is now no condemnation for those who are in Christ Jesus." Yet my belief system would not accept this plain truth. I believed Paul's words were for those who had their lives in order. Someday this verse might apply to me. But like a dangling carrot, freedom in Christ remained out of reach.

Condemnation was like a two-sided T-shirt I didn't realize I was wearing. The front said, "How am I doing?" The back said, "I'll try harder."

Like a wandering transient, I didn't fit in the world anymore but wasn't really cleaned up enough for heaven. I stood at heaven's gate with my cardboard sign—Will Work for God's Approval—a walking advertisement of defeated Christianity.

Though I knew my past sins were forgiven, I mistakenly believed my good works maintained my salvation. At the very least, they added some insurance—a reasonable assumption. But in truth, it was a powerful lie that had crystallized into a core belief, and everything I continued to learn about God passed through the grid of this flawed theology.

During these years, I often read Oswald Chambers's devotional, *My Utmost for His Highest*. The title summed up the intensity I required of myself. Even the language of the book reinforced the "up-to-me" belief system, through no fault of the author:

> "My determined purpose is to be my utmost for His highest—my best for His glory." To reach that level of determination is a matter of the will, not of debate or of reasoning.… But the acid test is obedience…in the details of our everyday life—sixty seconds out of every minute, and sixty minutes out of every hour.[2]

Chambers was *not* to blame for my spiritual condemnation. But without a foundation of grace, his ideas were twisted marching orders, placing me on a religious treadmill I didn't know how to exit. I felt weighed down by all the energy it took to be a good Christian.

I don't mean to say that taking pains to live for God doesn't matter. It does matter. But all our efforts should be in the context of a secure relationship. Condemnation creates an insecure relationship with God, and in that condition, any sense of connection with him is stifled.

Like many Christians, I had begun working *for* God's love instead of working *from* it as a basis of security. I didn't understand that grace is the centerpiece of Christian theology.

As I helped my daughter study for her world history exam, I realized that the cloud of condemnation hung over others as well. In prereformation days, clergy sold "indulgences" to churchgoers. Many believed this paid for their sins and released them from temporal punishment. Clearly this episode of church history repeated the scene of the money-changers whom Jesus rebuked. Yet people paid the church because they wanted that clean-slate feeling with God.

Joan of Arc provides another example. She made a statement during her trial that her prosecutors used to set a trap. She said, "Without the Grace of God I could do nothing." One priest asked, "Are you in a state of grace?" Immediately, Jean Lefevre, an honorable judge, cried out, "It is a terrible question! The accused is not obliged to answer it!" Everyone listened for her answer because it was considered presumptuous for anyone to believe he or she was fully accepted by God. No one knew for sure about making it to heaven. Joan, unruffled by the taunt, gave an immortal answer: "If I be not in a state of Grace, I pray God place me in it; if I be in it, I pray God keep me so." Though she answered humbly and wisely, her words reflected the felt uncertainty.[3]

I watched a documentary on TV of the Waco disaster. A closer look at David Koresh and the Branch Davidian tragedy of 1993 revealed condemnation themes. Members were taught that Christ died for the sins of earlier people, but not for them. Their salvation depended on their own efforts to obey Christ, which meant following the current prophet— David Koresh. Seventy-five people died in a raging fire, believing their obedience gave them standing with God.[4]

As I studied world religions, I found that condemnation is a universal experience. People in most every culture feel "the disappointment of the gods" and are compelled to make sacrifices or some form of appeasement as a way of life. How far will someone go to pay for sin? For example, I heard a news story about an Israeli taxi driver who was hospitalized after being stabbed by two Palestinian youths. The youths said the attack was their way to "repent of their sins." Not sure if God likes you today? Try stabbing someone. This makes no sense at all.

Hindus believe that if they fail to be good enough, the gods will demote them in the next life, and they may get stuck in an endless cycle of reincarnation. Buddhists have to become good enough for the afterlife by following the Noble Eightfold Path. But even if they've tried their level best, no certainty of heaven accompanies them into death.

The consequences of failure in the Islamic faith are the most alarming. Muslims are required to complete the Five Pillars of Islam, which involve daily recitations, praying five times a day, giving of alms, fasting during Ramadan, and a pilgrimage to Mecca. Marvin Olasky of *World Magazine* noted that beyond the pillars,

> Islamic scholars have developed an enormous list of what to do
> and what not to do—and that raises the question of what happens
> to those who break some rules. Many Muslims are relaxed about
> that, content that the 'five pillars of Islam'...will cover over a mul-
> titude of sins. But some become frenzied when they break the
> rules—and there are so many to break. Among some, that leads to
> a search for a 'get out of jail free' card—if there is such a thing.[5]

Allegedly, you can strap on a bomb and compensate for all your failures in one blazing act. Martyrdom has become yet another solution to
the trap of condemnation. Clearly, the struggle to be free from guilt and
shame is a deep human problem.

I'd been a Christian for almost twenty years before I understood the
fallout of condemnation in my own life. Truth finally came in a moment
of revelation. At the time I was a discussion leader in a large interdenominational Bible study. I remember sitting in a circle of women at the
leader's meeting contemplating Paul's words in Romans 8:15–16. Suddenly, God hit the pause button on my life, though the world continued
on. Without explanation, the discussion around me faded as the Holy
Spirit spoke fresh meaning into the few verses on the page before me:

> For you did not receive a spirit that makes you a slave again to
> fear, but you received the Spirit of sonship. And by him we cry,
> "Abba, Father." The Spirit himself testifies with our spirit that we
> are God's children. (NIV)

How did I miss this simple, straightforward passage? God was good.
He did not condemn us. His tenderness came through the words to me

like a gentle hand lifting my chin. Something deep inside me relaxed as I leaned back in my chair. God's soothing presence covered me like warm sunshine, breaking through years of grayness. That very day, a metamorphosis took place in my spiritual understanding. I truly couldn't deny his love for me. No longer would I abdicate my place as God's daughter. I'd felt a new certainty that his love was unconditional and everlasting.

My form of condemnation was rooted in a self-imposed perfectionism and a fixation on certain scriptures. For you, a father wound might be the disconnecting factor—it's just too hard to believe God loves you as you are. For others, the source might be a past moral failure that looms so large in their own minds—they don't see how could God possibly forgive them. Still another could be ensnared in addiction, and persistent failure may keep this one far from feeling God's affection. Whatever the origin, the lie of condemnation is insidiously destructive in its subtleties and may be the biggest obstacle preventing intimacy with God.

God brought me revelatory freedom through a few verses. After that day, a block was removed, and I stepped into an ongoing experience of God's love. It's not that his love wasn't there all along; condemnation blocked my reception.

In other scriptures, God showed me that Christianity was a kingdom built on love, not fear. When I accepted by faith the death of Christ as payment for my sins—past, present, *and future*—I entered the steadfast commitment of a Father-and-child relationship.

I am a work in progress and always will be. Yet God embraces me in my immaturity and watches my growth. He trains and disciplines me from the premise that my sin nature is a given. God knows the difference between a person who struggles to overcome sin and one who practices it—an outright hypocrite. I observed how differently Jesus treated the Pharisees, versus Peter who denied him or Thomas who doubted him. My standing and my future are secure, because God is the author and finisher of my faith. He is watching over my spirituality even when I'm not, and more important, when I can't.[6]

True condemnation from God comes when someone rejects Christ. It's not a matter of how perfectly you live the Christian life. Yet condemnation still hovers over many believers.

What's more, the negativity of guilt and shame breeds anger and disappointment toward God. That's the flip side of condemnation. Philip Yancey says this happens to countless people. Their disappointment is emotional, not intellectual. They may rant, "How do you *know* God's love is real?" But appealing to them with logic doesn't answer their question. Yancey concludes that emotional disappointment stems from the teaching that Christianity is a "relationship, not a religion," and many are not experiencing the relationship as promised.[7]

How does a finite person develop a connection with an infinite, invisible Being? Read the Bible, pray, take communion, worship harder? The attempts can all feel unreciprocated.

After the evening at church when the speaker asked three questions about God's love, I realized it doesn't matter if you believe God is love in theory. It also doesn't matter if you believe God loves you personally. Something more is essential. Biblical truth has little impact on your life if you aren't experiencing God's love.

In the award-winning movie *Blood Diamond,* a culminating scene demonstrates the power of a father's love to overcome his son's condemnation. If you've seen it, you know the heartbreaking reality all too commonplace in Africa: the tragedy of child soldiers.

Solomon Vandy's son, Dia, is abruptly conscripted one day by a rebel army as he walks home from school. Brutalized and brainwashed, Dia becomes a hardened killer in a meaningless war. Finding Dia becomes Solomon's obsession, and he decides to use a rare pink diamond as leverage with the rebel army. He knows his own life is in grave danger when he finds the rebel encampment.

The boys' camp is a modern day *Lord of the Flies*. Their eyes have seen too much. Drunk and drugged up, the boys dance with a gun in one hand, a beer in the other. Some smoke cigarettes and gamble under dim lights, awaiting their next siege.

When Solomon precariously rescues Dia, they flee to a hillside where the diamond lays buried. As Solomon unearths the stone, Dia raises a gun intending to kill the man who helped them.

Solomon looks up. "Dia, what are you doing? Dia, look at me. Look at me!" The boy shifts the gun toward his father. Maybe he wonders if his father is really after the diamond. Or could it be that Dia feels overwhelming shame as a rebel soldier? He can't return to normalcy with all the condemnation he bears.

Solomon slowly rises to his feet. The boy's lifeless eyes stare back at Solomon. Solomon calls to the boy he believes is still alive in Dia. With kindness, he speaks, gradually moving toward his son.

"You are Dia Vandy of the proud Mende tribe." The gun is now at point blank range, but Solomon is undaunted. "You are a good boy who loves soccer and school. Your mother loves you so much." Solomon's voice cracks with emotion. Dia's breathing is labored, but he says nothing. "She waits by the fire…making plantains and red palm oil stew…with your sister N'Yanda…and the new baby." The father weeps but doesn't take his eyes off his son. A small tear rolls down Dia's cheek, but he still holds the gun on his father.

"The cows wait for you," Solomon says. "And Babu, the wild dog who minds no one but you." The hardness over the son softens, and a stifled whimper escapes his throat. Anguish runs deep in his young soul.

Solomon steps closer, seeing the change in Dia's face. "I know they made you do bad things…but you are not a bad boy." With tender authority his words open a door of freedom. "I am your father…who loves you…and you will come home with me…and be my son again."

Tears flow now as Dia lowers his gun. Such a love is hard to believe, and he is troubled by it. But Solomon touches his head and pulls him into his embrace, his strong hand caressing Dia's face. The shadows of doubt have fled.[8]

How deep and high, far and wide is the love of God. Your Father knows that you have succumbed to the rebel-army nature of sin. Hurtful things were done to you, but you also made choices. The Father goes to the ends of the earth to rescue you, to tell you who you *really* are, and to bring you home. He risked his life in doing so. In fact, he gave his life. But now his forgiveness is complete, and he welcomes you into his embrace.

So many of God's own people don't know they are his beloved—and this is the church's greatest deficit. They lack the fullness of God's love and, therefore, deprive others, for they cannot offer what they do not have. Are you one of those who don't understand God's love? God wants us to come into a new place of understanding, agreeing with the disciple who said:

How great is the love the Father has lavished on us, that we should be called children of God! *And that is what we are!*[9]

SEVEN

Exposing Martha
A Lifestyle of Overdoing

*We are so obsessed with doing that we have no time
and no imagination left for being.*

—THOMAS MERTON

One summer our family participated in a program called Friendly Town. As an outreach to inner-city kids in Cleveland, a suburban family "adopts" an underprivileged kid for a week to broaden the child's life experience. We were assigned a young boy named Buddy who lived along the Cuyahoga River near the Flats in the old industrial part of Cleveland.

One Saturday morning, my parents asked my brother, my sister, and me to gather some personal belongings we didn't need anymore. After rummaging through our clothes and toys, we helped my parents load up our yellow Oldsmobile. Then we headed downtown. On the way, my father quietly told us to lock our doors. This stunned me. We had never been anywhere that wasn't safe.

The scenery out my window gradually changed like a moving mural. We left neighborhoods of manicured lawns, four-bedroom homes, and children riding bicycles. The roads doubled in size as we headed downtown. Soon I saw dilapidated buildings surrounded with dandelions and bits of trash. A booze bottle wrapped in a paper bag sat on the curb. Our car slowed to a stop, and we got out, collecting our sacks of hand-me-downs. Again, my father locked the car.

The apartment building smelled like a mildewed kitchen rag as we entered the stairwell. Dim lighting barely outlined a stairway that was steeper than normal and creaked under our weight. I walked into Buddy's small living quarters feeling like an intruder. For some reason, it felt rude to even look around the room, but I noticed a pot on the stove with a soup bone simmering on low.

We laid our bags of used offerings on their small kitchen table. My father carried the conversation, but our stay was brief. After a good-bye scene between Buddy and his mother, we headed down the dark steps to the car. Finally, I could breathe again.

Buddy seemed happy to go on this adventure. He was only six or seven but never acted homesick. He slept in the extra twin bed in my brother's third-floor room, wetting the sheets every night to my mother's chagrin. We took him everywhere, but he especially liked the swimming pool at the Yacht Club, because we bought him french fries and ice cream sandwiches at the snack bar. Though he lived in Cleveland, he had never seen Lake Erie. I laughed at the thought until my parents explained the confinement of poverty and inner-city life. Buddy's time with us lasted only a week, but my view of the world had been jarred.

Buddy stared at things in this new world of the suburbs. He didn't look at me with disdain, but after meeting him and seeing his home, I believed the poor, excluded, bitter ones of the earth were watching me. I saw "the look" on faces in the newspaper or on street people as I walked around downtown with my father. Sometimes I found their gaunt features and bitter stares in *National Geographic* or on TV. There were people who didn't have what I had, and this bothered me intensely. Some kind of injustice was at work in the world. And so, as time went on, I made a vow that *something must be done.*

Authors John and Paula Sandford in *The Transformation of the Inner Man* say that inner vows set a direction in someone's life the way railroad tracks determine the course of a train. An internal pronouncement of one's will powerfully influences perceptions and subsequent choices. Though a person may never even say a vow out loud, it's just as potent. Vows are often made by people in deep pain, with words like "I will always…" and "Never again…" phrases.[1] My inner vow as a youth did not come from my pain, but from the awareness that others were in pain. Later, as I read Jesus's plea to care for the "least of these," my inner vow to fix the world became galvanized.

I started to see people differently. I felt terrible shame about Fergus, the boy we ridiculed on our tour bus in Europe. I noticed girls who didn't get asked to dance at parties. I made a point to say hi to the kids in school who had horrible acne. I studied the face of Barbara, our cleaning lady, as she worked around our house, wondering what her life was like when she got on the bus to go home. I befriended the kid everyone said was a "narc," when the ninth-grade potheads terrorized him and chased him all the way home. I baked him a cake when he told me his mother hated him.

The lighthearted days of my childhood were quickly fading away. The happy little girl became a melancholy, contemplative teenager, who sometimes gave way to pessimism. I was slow to laugh with any kind of abandon, and it wasn't just adolescent moodiness.

Up to me. Never good enough. Something must be done. Have you ever stopped to notice the tapes that play over and over in your head? I hadn't, and I didn't know enough to know that I should. I kept most of my thoughts to myself, and of course, that was part of the problem.

I saw a movie once where a lady says to the person next to her, "Is the noise inside my head bothering you?" The comment reminded me of the ongoing questions raging in my thoughts day and night: Why is the world so messed up? What should I do about it? Does anything matter?

Where is God in all of this? Does he care about injustice? Most of the time, I factored God out of the solution. Human beings had made a mess of things, so we had better fix them before God gives up on us.

But here's the rub: if you could have turned my savior's complex inside out, you would have seen that the driving force behind it all was self-preservation. I was busy earning my way into God's favor, and the duty of religiosity and insecurity of condemnation kept the fires burning.

Recently I watched *Saving Private Ryan.*[2] In the film, a platoon of soldiers sets out on a mission to find a particular soldier in the French countryside. Government officials maintain Private Ryan must return home immediately, because all three of his brothers have already been killed in action. Military leaders want to spare his family the grief of losing all their sons. The soldiers have mixed feelings about their mission. One by one, most of them are killed, but eventually they find their man.

In a closing scene, the captain of the platoon lies dying after a brutal assault by the enemy. Private Ryan finds the mortally wounded leader in the rubble. In his final words, the captain looks up and says to Ryan, "Earn this." Inherent in his words is the thought that because many died to save his life, he must in turn live as one worthy of their sacrifice. Ryan accepts his noble request. After that, the scene transforms to the future where a very old Private Ryan stands at the grave of the captain, asking his wife if he had been a good man—good enough.

As a young Christian, my misunderstanding of the cross could have used the same script. In my mind, I saw Jesus hanging on the cross, with me, a trembling bystander, looking on. I imagined Jesus lifting his head, looking at me with penetrating eyes as he said his parting words—"Earn this." I must live worthy of his sacrifice. At first glance, it seems like sound theology, but the notion is flawed. No one can earn it. No life can match the gift.

A poignant scene from the 1973 movie *Papillon*[3] also reinforced my thinking during these years. The story centers on a Frenchman, Henri Charrière, played by Steve McQueen. Wrongly convicted of murder,

Charrière is shipped to the French Guiana prison complex, where he will inevitably suffer the inhumane aspects of prison life. During a period of solitary confinement, he has a surreal vision involving a desert scene where he sees his own judgment day before a panel of judges. He walks toward them when suddenly the chief justice yells out:

"You know the charge."

Charrière stops walking and yells back, "I'm innocent! I didn't kill that pimp. You couldn't get anything on me and you framed me!"

"That is quite true," declares the judge, to Charrière's surprise. He continues, "But your real crime has nothing to do with a pimp's death!"

"Well then, what is it?"

"Yours is the most terrible crime a human being can commit." Charrière waits in dread and silence until the judge resumes. "I accuse you of a wasted life." The judge's words impact the accused with visible force.

Charrière lowers his head and quietly says to himself, "Guilty."

"The penalty for that is death!" the judge shouts with finality.

Charrière turns and slowly walks away saying, "Guilty," over and over.

As I watched this scene, another inner-vow kind of moment transpired. *I will never be guilty of a wasted life* were my exact thoughts. And so my will, like a locked steering wheel, set a course for a performance-oriented life. I embarked on the road to being a Martha.[4]

My something-must-be-done mandate began with inner-city projects with Teen OutReach through Christian Help (TORCH). On Saturdays, along with other teens, my sister and I cleaned house for the old, sick people in urban Cleveland. For three summers I served on the volunteer staff of two different Young Life camps. Later I worked with senior citizens in my first full-time job. I also packed food boxes, washed vegetables, and sorted stale bread donations at the local Food Bank, seeing the face of hunger up close. I befriended several homeless women and tried to help them reenter life—find a place to live, purchase some furnishings, and build the courage to apply for jobs. This involved many hours and extended phone conversations.

I worked in the personnel field for over ten years, which involved counseling and administrative work. I became a Young Life leader and served on the Young Life Committee, leading teen Bible studies and organizing fund-raisers. For many years, I cooked for a college youth group's annual three-day retreat with over 120 students attending. I know this all sounds admirable, like a life full of purpose, but things aren't what they seem. My works theology got much worse.

As I grew older, my attention shifted from the poor, excluded ones to the bitter ones, wounded by life. Some of this shift took place when I joined Bible Study Fellowship as a leader. For four years, I always asked for "little knowledge" groups, women who were new to Christianity or had minimal exposure to the Bible. Those relationships involved more care and more time to answer questions. I was asked to make a ten-minute call to each woman, every week, for the entire nine months of the study. But minutes turned to hours as women poured out their pain. I usually had between fifteen and seventeen women in my group. You can imagine how my phone time multiplied. To complicate matters, each fall I received a new group of women, but kept friendships alive from previous groups. By the end of four years, I had relationships with over fifty women.

At the same time, my friend Jenny and I started a prayer-counseling ministry under my pastor's guidance. We talked and prayed with a different person every week for four years. Our sessions lasted three to four hours. Many of these people were severely wounded and contacted us through word-of-mouth connections. We addressed situations of divorce, abandonment, incest, abuse, adultery, addiction, marital conflict, parenting stress, and bereavement. We prayed with a woman who grew up in a satanic cult, a man dying of AIDS, a man with multiple personalities, and a woman whose daughter had been murdered.

In the meantime, my husband and I hosted a home group Bible study every week. We converted our horse barn into a guesthouse to provide a place of rest for people in full-time ministry. Local pastors as well as missionaries and conference speakers from all over the world used the guesthouse. It called for a tremendous amount of housekeeping. Besides all this, I worked on countless school projects, church committees, community needs, and carried almost all of the domestic responsibilities of maintaining a sizable home, yard, and garden. And did I forget to mention caring for my three small children?

During these manic years, exhaustion was a way of life. I would get a cold and not get over it for months. One whole summer I experienced seizurelike symptoms that puzzled the specialists. The manifestations were warning signs of stress, but my overcommitted life kept me racing from one thing to the next.

I was chronically late. I had several to-do lists in several places. You would often find me folding laundry, paying bills, or balancing the checkbook late at night. Our phone became a crisis hotline. It was not unusual to have over twenty calls a day. I started hating the sound of the phone ringing.

In some ways, I really stopped caring about people. To avoid running into someone I knew at the grocery, I shopped at odd hours of the day. Sometimes I would quickly change aisles to avoid conversation. On a good day, a lot of things got checked off my lists. A bad day involved unexpected setbacks as simple as the dog running off in the neighborhood. My marginless life had become a prescription for burnout.

Looking back, I deeply regret how this affected my family. I felt anxious when my children became sick, because it put me behind. A glass of spilled milk could set off my temper. I even felt mad when the cats meowed for their food. My husband described me as an Everready Christian—one who keeps going, going, going. My lifestyle undoubtedly created some loneliness in our marriage.

One night after tucking the kids in bed, my husband and I gathered up LEGOs pieces scattered all over the living room floor. As we tossed them into their container, my husband mischievously threw one at me. At first I ignored it, but after a moment, another one clipped my shoulder.

"Stop it," I muttered. I was dead on my feet and just wanted to go to bed. A third building block hit me in the head. Now I was annoyed. "Just quit it, would you!" I said sharply. He said nothing but glumly sat there. Finally I looked up and said, "What…what is it?"

He paused at first, then said, "I just wanted you to throw one back."

In the driven quest to be selfless, good, and productive, it's easy to forget how to live. I felt cranky and empty. Looking in the mirror I saw dark circles under the eyes of a very tired woman. My shoulders slumped as I exhaled deep feelings of fatigue. An aching knot in my stomach would not go away. Its tightening grip was cumulative and had become my constant companion.

Who was I? I was a full-blown Martha. How could all my good intentions and noble beliefs produce such a train-wreck life? It's a quick-sand problem for many Christians, eating up time for healthy relation-ships, especially with God. One of the forms of religiosity, the syndrome is fueled by condemnation. A driven lifestyle can be window-dressed as "spiritual," but it's often a form of pain avoidance. And pain was the last and hardest obstacle I'd have to overcome.

EIGHT

Ambushed by Life
The Insolent Conundrum of Pain

*Anger is an acid that
can do more harm to
the vessel in which it is
stored than to anything
on which it is poured.*

—MARK TWAIN

A few days ago, a guy yelled at me as I walked up to make a deposit at the bank. Apparently, he felt I took his place in line when he stopped to fill out his deposit slip at the counter. When he saw me completing my slips at the teller window, he started ranting.

"Hey lady! I stopped here to not hold up the line! Where do you get off?" His angry words shattered the silence in a place as quiet as a library. I was stunned. He didn't know I needed information from the teller to complete my slips. By now, a line had formed, creating an audience for this unpleasant scene.

"I'm sorry," I said softly, turning to look at him directly. "I didn't know what you were doing at the counter." He moaned and muttered a few choice words.

The same week, an elderly neighbor backed out of her driveway and hit a parked car belonging to my daughter's friend. The woman was livid when I called the police. The car was already being reviewed by an insurance company for damage from another incident. This second accident could make negotiations between insurance companies somewhat dicey. I had to report it. Feeling criminalized, my neighbor worried that the police would be knocking on her door any day to take away her license. No matter how I tried to console her, she remained argumentative. Her fury seemed out of proportion to the situation.

People are on edge everywhere. Road rage, school violence, small town disputes, political rivalries. We pop off at others to diffuse the pain in our own lives. A random circumstance can trigger a kick-the-dog response toward the nearest bystander. Hostility comes out sideways, hurting others unjustly.

But it can also turn inward. Repressed anger and pain can become a sorrow leading to depression, suicide, addictions, eating disorders, and other crippling problems. "The heart knows its own bitterness,…when the heart is sad, the spirit is broken."[1] Whether anger is expressed overtly or turned inward, someone gets hurt, because the real problem often isn't the incident at hand.

How many people are willing to explore the true sources of their anger? Is their frustration really about a parked car or a lady at the bank? Not usually. Getting angry about stuff that doesn't matter is a symptom of deeper pain with things that really do matter. At the core, anger is often tied to relational pain. It's a cover-up. Essentially, we've been hurt by someone. Over time, unresolved pain goes unhealed and accumulates, causing strife and estrangement. Anger is a common response to pain we don't know how to deal with.

Anger is also circumstantial. Maybe you just received a cancer diagnosis or your business went bankrupt. Or perhaps you're just mad because your car wouldn't start. Whether it's relational or circumstantial, a *why me?* feeling rises up. Behind the question may be an urge to shake your fist at heaven.

Underneath all the everyday pain, many people feel anger toward God. But the anger is unconscious; we think it's forbidden, something only atheists dare to feel. Let's face it—being mad at God is hard to acknowledge. If you did, you might get struck by lightning, or the earth might open up and swallow you. Yet if God is so powerful and knows all about the troubles in the world, why doesn't he do something to fix our pain and suffering? Don't you wonder?

I have.

When pain ambushed my life as a wife and young mother, I qualified for the shaking-of-the-fist camp. I think my response was partly because my childhood was so safe and idyllic. When adulthood arrived in my early twenties, I was like a little hothouse flower set outside in the raw elements. The wind, frost, and scorching sun came, and I didn't fare so well.

Some of the most difficult pain entered my life through a door called marriage. Marriage is a testing ground, a refining fire for everyone who takes the journey. Of course, some suffering in marriage is a dying-to-self kind of pain that builds character. As a new bride, I accepted that part of "for better or for worse." But I didn't plan on the heartache of betrayal and rejection.

Duncan's affair seven years into our marriage left me completely shredded. Dejection hung on me like a millstone. I wanted to disappear or run away, but concern for my two-year-old daughter kept me from being rash. I was also pregnant. We stayed together, seeing counselors and pastors, but the road ahead proved difficult.

Superficially, life went on, and Sarah was born. Soon we became adept at playing house for the benefit of our young daughters. Like two strangers who were once intimately acquainted, we practiced detached cordiality. Outwardly, we wore our rings, but internally we drifted toward what author John Sandford calls a "silent divorce." [2]

During this time, my husband came to terms with his alcoholism and genuinely found God. [3] Still, the early years of his sobriety were volatile, making everything in the family unstable. At times, I got on the emotional roller coaster with him, not understanding how his alcoholism affected me.

As I learned about substance abuse in Al-Anon meetings, I found myself hopping mad at God. I slammed a few doors and screamed into my bed pillow. My turn-the-other-cheek, lay-down-your-life Christianity had become the perfect script for codependency. As the martyr, I played the traditional, nurturing role, which led to a dreadful free fall. I sacrificed my identity while my husband retreated deeper and deeper into self-absorption. Our broken relationship was textbook. The Christian way of life steered me straight into dysfunction, and I felt utterly hoodwinked by my own faith.

Until that time, I didn't really know God. I was religiously active, trapped in overdoing, and still suffocating under the lie of condemnation. In dutiful ways, I did all the nice things Christian people do, but as we know, self-reliant religion is a far cry from true faith.

But here's a little secret about pain. It serves a very important purpose.

Pain brought the tipping point. Adultery left an excruciating wound, potent enough to implode my life. Finally God had an opportunity to enter my insular world. A counselor later told me this was good—the upside of a marital shipwreck. If one piece of me had been left standing, I would have used it to rebuild the illusion that everything was okay. I would have continued living in my own strength. Deep suffering took away that false pride and smashed the walls that kept me from God.

In a way, Duncan's moral failure and alcoholism were just triggers. My marital pain was real, but only a small part of what God was after. God was provoking a much deeper pain to come up and out of me. In the most loving terms, he was saying, "Come on, Susan, get *really* angry! Take a swing at me! I can handle it."

Picture a little kid who has lost his temper and is swinging wildly at his father. The father stands calmly, with his hand on his son's forehead, gently holding him at arm's length. The father is patient and full of love as the boy releases his frustration, mostly hitting air. After a while, the boy winds down, his anger subsides, and soon he falls into his father's embrace. The embrace couldn't happen otherwise. Acknowledging anger prevents it from going underground where it becomes dangerously divisive and forms deep roots.

God is that patient father. He was big enough to love Job when Job's pain brought a flurry of wild words. I'm not saying it's okay to curse God. But to never admit to God that you're frustrated or angry with him creates a barrier.

In J. D. Salinger's classic story, *Franny and Zooey,* the older brother, Buddy, sums up this principle in a letter to Zooey following their brother Seymour's suicide. He says, "You were the only one who was bitter...and the only one who really forgave him for it. The rest of us...were outwardly unbitter and inwardly unforgiving."[4]

Wrenching pain brought devastation but also an opportunity for transformational change because I was in the hands of a loving Father. You see, it required me to get real with God. No charade of Christianity could mend my shattered world. No slogans, fix-it-all verses, or banal encouragement could reach me in my black hole of sorrow. Human counsel mattered little. Food tasted bland; sleep was restless at best. Day to day, I functioned mechanically at home and at work. I didn't want to go to church. I didn't want to read the Bible, and I *really* didn't want to pray. If you've ever known this kind of despondency, you also understand how powerless it feels. Mostly I felt confused.

For so long I had believed God was instrumental in bringing Duncan and me together. We dated in college but broke up our junior year. Alcoholic patterns were already evident in his life, and I couldn't take his wild behavior. But years later, after graduation, I was passing through Columbus, Ohio, in my grandparents' car. Duncan had just left a doctor's office, and we both pulled up to a stoplight at the same moment. The odds of this happening seemed astounding in a city of over a million people. And so, right or wrong, I assumed God himself had arranged our serendipitous reunion.

Fast forward seven years. Alcoholism and infidelity had come like a wrecking ball. I found myself questioning God. *Why God? Why this man? My life could have been so different.* Was God complicit in my unending pain? Questions boomeranged inside my head, and I heard no answer.

Eventually I found a book by Catherine Marshall called *Something More.* In it, she says love is stymied when "bitterness and resentment have slammed shut the door of the heart and unforgiveness stands as the sentinel at the door.... Forgiveness is the precondition of love."[5] She talked about choosing to do some *deliberate* forgiveness work.

This was a new idea to me. Each morning, Catherine and her husband, Leonard, spent thirty minutes separately asking God to show them any relationship where they harbored unforgiveness. Starting with their childhoods, they worked forward through different periods of their lives. When the half hour had passed, they met together and verbally forgave each person on their lists, releasing those hurts to God. Afterward, the pages were torn up and stored in a big envelope.

Their forgiveness work went on week after week and months on end. Eventually, after clearing out the debris of accumulated pain, they burned the envelope of torn pages, releasing it as a sacrifice to God. In return, they experienced the joy of reconciliation in several estranged relationships and the freedom of having a clean conscience before God.[6]

Their story completely leveled me. Jesus's mandate to forgive was not based on whether or not the offenders were sorry or whether they changed or any guarantee that they would never hurt another again. I didn't like that. I put conditions on my forgiveness toward others. But God's kingdom was different. The motivation to forgive was based on one thing: we forgive because God has forgiven us.[7] I found this challenging.

Forgiveness is not a sweet little gesture, like baking cookies for someone. It's completely antithetical to human nature. It's a decision that requires immense courage and faith. Think of a Jewish person forgiving a member of the Nazi regime or an African slave forgiving a slave trader. That conjures up quite a different picture. But for those who choose to, forgiveness is a dynamic spiritual force, releasing the very power of God to heal and restore.

In time, I agreed to try.

Following Catherine and Leonard's example, I set out to forgive my husband, writing page after page of stored up pain—far beyond the issue of infidelity. It was like cleaning out a storage closet full of junk; I didn't know how much was packed away until I brought it into the open. I wrote and wept and wrote some more. Grieving didn't feel productive at first. To this day, I'm not sure I agree with the idea of a "good" cry. I felt stuck in the viselike grip of an unending trial, but I kept writing. When the time was right, I confessed my hidden and not-so-hidden unforgiveness to a friend, releasing Duncan from my judgments and asking God to work in his life.

In time, I forgave others in my life as well—parents, siblings, friends, teachers, bosses, church leaders, and others—tearing up my papers into little pieces. The forgiveness work seemed exhaustive, but one day, a friend of mine pointed out that I had yet to forgive God.

"What? Are you kidding?" I laughed nervously. "But God hasn't done anything wrong."

"True, but you are mad at him," she said. I was shocked. Though I didn't like it, her comment struck a chord. The room grew very quiet. A burning sensation started on my neck and moved up face. After a moment, a big tear rolled down my hot cheek.

"It's true…" My words were muffled. "But how? Why?" I couldn't shut down my emotions now.

She reached for a Kleenex box.

"You're mad at God because you don't think he's doing a good job of being God. He's allowed unjust suffering in your life and in the lives of many around you: your husband's affair, a friend's suicide, even the fact that there are starving children in Africa." I wadded up a Kleenex and pressed it to my wet eyes. My head hung over my lap. "Susan, you're not sure God can be trusted, and you've put his heart on trial."

I nodded, but didn't look up. Why was this so scary to admit? She nailed it. How could she know all this? Christianity, I thought, had led me into dysfunction, but until then, I never connected with the fact that I was really angry with God.

Later that day, I started writing all the ways I felt God had failed to intervene in a broken world. Somehow I had made this my personal argument with him. Three hours went by, then four, followed by days and weeks. The Holy Spirit reminded me of countless scenes from the nightly news. Time and again something terrible had happened—a drought, a famine, an epidemic. Inside the fire raged. *What about that, God? How can things like that happen? What are you going to do about it?* I was ready to pick a fight, but he didn't respond in any way I recognized. Silently I added these kinds of things to an ongoing list in my heart. Resentments toward God had been building for years, perhaps since I met Buddy, our Friendly Town child. In all the forgiveness work I'd done, I'd left the biggest job for last.

I'll never forget the day I forgave God. This same friend helped me again. First I spoke a simple prayer. *"God, though you haven't done anything wrong, I admit I'm mad at you."* Then I confessed a long litany of resentments, one by one. My patient friend understood the importance of these admissions. When I finished, she prayed comforting words over me, but I don't remember a thing she said. I was too enthralled by the image forming in my mind.

You might call it a daydream, maybe a vision. All I know is that while my eyes were closed, I saw Jesus facing me at the other end of a teetertotter. Light emanated from him as he smiled. His eyes were beautiful. He looked down the plank at me, a little girl sitting at the low end with a large earthlike ball adding ballast to my side. At first, I didn't notice the heavy world in front of me. I was so taken with Jesus, enjoying the moment. I could hear a conversation going on:

"Let's play," Jesus said, chiding me to push up my end.

"I can't." I nodded toward the large globe in front of me.

He exhaled slightly and studied me with soft eyes. "It's not what you think. It's really light. And one day, I'll toss it away because it's not what's really important."

"Then what *is* really important?" I demanded.

"You and me."

I thought about that, looking up at his radiant face.

He continued. "I want to teach you to roll the world back and forth with me."

"What do you mean?" I asked, knowing it was too heavy.

"There will be times when the world is too great a burden for you, and I want you to roll the ball to me. Other times, I'll have something for you to do in the world, and I'll roll it back to you. But if you don't send it over to me now, we can't play."

This silent conversation was superimposed on a memory straight out of my childhood. My friends and I used to roll a ball back and forth on the teetertotter as we pushed up and down in rhythm. This time Jesus wanted to play. He longed to reframe my worldview and remind me that all of this is temporary.

Relationship with God is all important. One day, the earth will roll away like a beachball in the wind. What will remain? What is eternal? What makes the whole deal worth the suffering?

In a word: Jesus.

God had dissolved yet another barrier. My hidden rift had been exposed, and in a brief moment, completely resolved. It took a long time to forgive my husband and others, but those walls had come down. And that revealed my need to do the same with God.

When I admitted my frustration to God, he showed me the next step—a step of faith, to trust him no matter what it looks like here on earth. The hard-packed soil of my heart had been chisel-plowed; a root-bound field of bitterness had been broken up and turned over.

A perfectly prepared space was now ready for planting, and intimacy with God would be the harvest.

As my friend prayed for me on an ordinary afternoon, little did she realize it was an eternal shift in my life. And Jesus slipped in to share the moment.

NINE

_____

Inklings
Listening for God

If we pause to listen, we will discover how often God speaks to us through human and earthly means. He stands at the windows of the easily overlooked and the unlikely, tapping at the pane. He beckons us to

places of encounter where we learn how well he understands the language of our hearts.

—KEN GIRE, _WINDOWS OF THE SOUL_

There is no trick to hearing God's voice. It has nothing to do with the number of years someone's been a Christian. Nor is it about being more spiritual than another. Once the barriers are cleared away, it comes down to noticing things, taking a second look, and pausing to reflect.

I was already hearing his voice in Scripture. I knew he could take a childhood memory like playing on a teetertotter and create a visual message. My dreams seemed highly symbolic and fascinating. I could hear his still small voice in Christmas carols. Learning to recognize God's presence is just about connecting the dots. You might have an *aha* moment, like the feeling when you first learned to ride a bike without training wheels. But for me, the realization was a gradual dawning, a growing awareness that God had been there all along.

When I learned to sail, I spent several summers attending a sailing camp. My fellow campers and I studied the important terms: *bow, starboard, port, sheet, halyard, telltale, rudder,* and *tiller.* Our instructors drew illustrations on a chalkboard, sketching all the different angles the boat could be relative to the breeze. They showed us how to "tack," or sail in a zigzag approach toward the wind, and they explained the dynamics of charting a course when racing.

After we rigged our sails, a powerboat towed our little bathtub-sized boats down the Rocky River to Lake Erie. The waves were so intimidating that we promptly forgot everything we had just learned. As a ten-year-old, I was terrified the first few times on the lake. But eventually the instructions started making sense, and I calmed down.

I noticed the boat went faster if I pulled in the sail and pushed the tiller away from me slightly. This is called "heading up." If the breeze was too strong, I "spilled" wind by letting out the sail, simultaneously pulling the tiller closer to me.

When I sail today, I don't think about all those lessons learned long ago. On a gorgeous August day, I glide through sparkling water in a small, sleek boat, and it becomes an extension of my body. I read the approaching wind by looking for dark, rougher spots on the water. I pull the mainsail in and release it instinctively. When a puff of air comes, I lean out to counterbalance the tilt. My entire body flows in sync with the shift of the wind and its effect on the boat. Believe it or not, these are times of rest for me, because it's not a mind thing.

Anyone who's ever learned to play the piano knows what it's like to painstakingly memorize notes, timing, and syncopation. Initially it feels like patting your head and rubbing your stomach at the same time. But after a while, you finally learn a song or two. You reach a point where the mechanics fade away and the music takes over. If you think too hard about individual notes in a song, it messes you up. Some of this development in music just happens. I don't know how.

Maybe you don't sail or play the piano. But you know the transition I'm talking about if you've ever learned to type, paint a picture, or drive a car. You reach a stage where you know how to do something so well that you forget the specific steps. You leave the paint-by-numbers realm and enter a dynamic place where you sense and respond with a deep kind of knowing.

These examples form a picture of how one learns to hear God's voice. It evolves. You begin with the basics, like beginning anything else. If God is going to speak today in fresh ways, he will not contradict his established written Word. The more you know the Bible, the more vocabulary God has to work with. No one learns a new language without understanding terminology, context, symbols, metaphors, and in this case, the Author.

Pastors and teachers expand our understanding of God. Fellowship groups are another good forum for hearing how others experience God. We invite God's presence through prayer, worship, repentance, and humility. These things are important ingredients for intimacy with God. But ingredients do not make a cake. At some point, every believer must enter her own spiritual experience with God.

Often this is the point in the Christian journey where the mind gets in the way. We back away from the very situations in which God is trying to make contact, missing the moment, the message, and the mystery. Our heads overpower our hearts, taking charge of the situation. I'm not talking about laying aside wisdom and discernment. But some people have a mind-set that leaves no room for God to be God. Sometimes he has to circumvent our finite, systematic minds and our stubborn religious frameworks in order to speak to our hearts in the way deep calls to deep.

As a child, my openness to some kind of experience with God was unfettered. If God spoke to me in the lyrics of a Christmas carol, I received it as such, without analysis. But as you may recall, I was skeptical as a young adult. When people said things like, "God told me…" I wondered why God didn't tell *me*. It was downright perplexing. It seemed outlandish to make such a claim. Did God play favorites? Was I a second-class Christian if I didn't hear God? I accepted the fact that God spoke with people in the Bible, but God did speak, interact, and connect with people now—in real time? My intellectual mind argued with the idea, even though I longed for more than goose bumps and warm feelings on Christmas Eve. I wanted something beyond a tear or two over someone else's miraculous story. I had some inklings of God. Still, I wanted to grow in my capacity to hear him.

What did I have to *do*?

I had to believe it was possible and get quiet and calm enough to notice things. He was coaxing me into his presence with a series of small moves.

First he entered my pain. One morning, I curled up in a wing-backed chair, hugging my knees. Duncan had left for work, and the girls were still sleeping. A wave of grief came over me, and I'm not sure how long I wept. Though his affair was over and years had passed, our marriage was still fragmented. A friend called it a "pathological separation." But God showed up that morning, flowing like soothing oil through the cracks of my brokenness.

Before long, I noticed a song playing over and over in my head, like a radio tune stuck on replay. It seemed hymnlike. I followed the melody to the refrain and then remembered the title: "Great Is Thy Faithfulness."[1] We had an old hymnbook in the piano bench, so I looked up the lyrics. Certain phrases came alive, as if God were speaking them directly to me. The lyrics seemed to hold a message just for me. In everyday language it sounded like this:

I'm here for you, Susan. My love for you doesn't change. Every morning new things will happen to show you I'm at work. I will provide all that you need. I'm coming with you, to comfort you and show you which way to go. I'll give you strength today and hope for your future. I can give you a lasting peace. I'm here for you.

The song entered my mind from nowhere. It was quiet, almost imperceptible, and easily could have been ignored. I can't recall how many years had passed since I had sung this song in church. Remember, I was never much of a hymn singer. But God can use anything, even experiences that seemed religious and uninspiring at the time.[2] The lyrics were more powerful than ever before. Now, looking back, I realize the Holy Spirit was singing to me, drawing me out of my all-encompassing pain and comforting me like no other could.

The Lord continued to make contact with me. A week or so later, my daughter came home from Sunday school with a verse for the day: "Is anything too difficult for the LORD?"[3] As I read it, I sensed God was asking me that question. The next day, while driving to town, a guy on the radio quoted the exact same verse. Again God caught my attention, speaking one way, then another.

God was overcoming the walls I had constructed to keep him away. I didn't want any false hope. I didn't want to hurt anymore. Nevertheless, he patiently pursued me, consoling my broken heart.

Next I came across a startling verse in the Old Testament. The words held a certain intimacy: "For the LORD has called you, like a wife forsaken and grieved in spirit."[4] He spoke like a friend who knows the hidden tears and untold sorrow.

Then one night I had a dream.

I'm walking briskly down a poorly lit hallway when my left hand inadvertently slams against a wooden chair. My fingers smart with pain.

Looking closer at my hand, I notice the blow has knocked the solitaire diamond out of my wedding ring. The empty setting looks ugly. To me it symbolized the duty of marriage without the beauty.

"Who cares? Marriage is a failed experiment anyway," I say, but I wince. My voice sounds morosely satisfied with a heartless existence. I continue down the hallway. "Whatever," I mutter under my breath. But a part of me wants to look for the diamond. I pause in a moment of vacillation.

Returning to the wooden chair, I kneel down, groping for the tiny stone in the dim light. To my surprise, I feel many small angular rocks. With a sweeping motion, I gather some to get a better look. Catching my breath, I find a handful of beautifully cut crystals—sapphire blue, emerald green, and deep purple. In the middle of all the gems lies the original diamond. It looks tiny in comparison, yet it sparkles in the faint light. I know something meaningful is happening. I'm supposed to take all the stones to Duncan for a new wedding ring. Something of greater value will be restored.

When morning came, I rested peacefully in my bed for a long time. A spiritual sneeze moment had transpired. The dream was linked to a small miracle in my past. In the early years of our marriage, four years before the affair, I actually lost the diamond in my wedding ring. It happened one spring day as I worked in the sandy dirt of our backyard garden.

On that day, I threw on a clean white T-shirt and my favorite old jeans with holes in the knees. It was such a beautiful morning. I felt antsy to get outside as I waited for the slowest coffeepot in the world. Finally, with digging implements in hand, I pushed open the gate of a wire fence that surrounded the garden area. I set my steaming coffee on top of a wooden corner post and laid a bottle of ice water in the shade. Thrusting the shovel into the ground, I grimaced when it only penetrated about two inches. Fortunately we had a pickax. After hours of digging, picking, and raking, I had harvested a small mountain of rocks.

My shoulders felt sunburned, but thick white clouds would soon block the sweltering sun.

Laying the shovel down, I reached for the ice water and lost my balance in a moment of vertigo. I grabbed the fence to stabilize my spinning world. The horizon eventually returned to its place, and I let go of the fence but simultaneously heard a tiny pling sound of metal against metal. Instinctively, I looked at my wedding ring. The six-prong setting held nothing. The diamond had catapulted into the air.

My heart fluttered like a frightened bird. Forcefully extending my arms, I commanded the world to be still. Our cat, Puddy, quickly snuck under the deck. My diamond was a third-generation heirloom from my husband's family. But out of its setting, it was just one more tiny pebble in a large, rocky garden.

"Oh God…" I prayed breathlessly. Scanning the landscape at my feet, I hoped beyond hope something would sparkle and catch my eye. A few cumulus clouds drifted over, hiding the sun. *What will I do?* Paralyzed, I waited statuelike for something to happen.

Finally, sunbeams returned like a spotlight, and in my peripheral vision I saw a tiny flicker of light. Rotating in slow motion toward the twinkling source, I inched closer. The prepared soil shifted like sand under my feet. The diamond could so easily disappear with any movement of the dirt. Taking shallow breaths, I stared at the glimmering dot, determined not to even blink. I carefully got down on all fours, moving forward like a cat on the scent of a mouse. Finally, I reached for the little clear stone. My fingers felt the sharp edge of a cut diamond. I rolled it over in my sweaty palm and watched the sun refract a thousand little lights through the crystal. A rush of heat filled my cheeks. *You gave it back to me!* Silently I thanked God.

Finding my lost diamond seemed like nothing short of a miracle. And God used a dream to remind me. The backyard incident was more than happenstance—now it was a miracle with a message. He knew adultery would rip my marriage apart like a diamond wrenched from its setting. He knew I would stay married out of commitment, without the joy, like a ring with empty prongs. But in the garden, he demonstrated rather dramatically that he was able to fully restore my marriage. I only understood the symbolism in retrospect. The dream made the link.

God...you'll help me? I asked, lying under the covers. For so long, pain had dominated my world, yet it had brought me closer to the heart of God. He became real, present in my suffering. He wanted me to know he was there.

Just as a baby doesn't speak in complete sentences, learning to hear God and communicate with him didn't start with amazing revelations. In this instance, a familiar melody played in my head. I noticed it. I read my daughter's Sunday school verse and heard it again on the radio. I felt God's stirrings. Other verses seemed astonishingly specific to my situation. I wrote them in a journal. Soon after, I had a dream with symbolic implications. The dream led to a memory of an unbelievable scene in my backyard. With new understanding, I saw the significance of finding my diamond. All I had to do was pause, get quiet enough to ponder, and let God weave it all together for me.

How easy it would have been to ignore God's moves as nothing more than random circumstances, shooing them away like pesky flies. I could have sat in that wing-backed chair and cried all day. I could have read my daughter's Bible verse and mindlessly said, "That's nice, honey." I could have dismissed the guy on the radio, stopped reading my Bible, and disregarded the dream. Maybe I was just lucky when I found my diamond years ago in the sandy dirt.

For years I did snub the small inklings of the Holy Spirit, like flicking pieces of lint off my collar. But this time I stopped, noticed, and waited for God to make sense of his overtures. I dialed down my noisy mind and allowed his presence to enter my world.

Had I only known what I was missing. How warm and soothing it is to sense God's touch, his nearness, and his love. I could feel the strain in my neck muscles relax, the stress drain from my mind. An unexpected tranquillity comes when you know God is utterly aware of your life, sees what you see, and feels what you feel, but always has a much larger story in mind for you. It was as though I had crossed some invisible threshold.

Moses crossed this kind of threshold on a very ordinary day. While shepherding his father-in-law's flocks, he saw a burning bush. You know the story, but the text says he turned and *looked*. He took time to observe. "I will go over and see this strange sight," he said. "When the LORD saw that he had gone over to look, God called to him."[5] It's as simple as that. When we stop, wait, notice, and listen, God speaks. Our ability to hear him intensifies as we learn to recognize his voice in everyday circumstances. When he knows we're listening, he communicates in greater measure.[6]

"Indeed God speaks once, or twice, yet no one notices it."[7] The question is—will we listen?

TEN

Puzzles
God Speaks in Metaphors and Mysteries

The secret things belong to the LORD our God,
but the things revealed belong to us.
—MOSES, DEUTERONOMY 29:29

I n our family, we call them "blue-green days." We know the exact meaning of this phrase, though it's challenging to explain our collective experience to others.

Blue-green days happen in a specific place called the French River in northern Ontario. You'd have to experience it to fully understand the mystique. In fact, I can't imagine a blue-green day in another part of the world. At the very least, I'd have to call it something else.

A blue-green day on the French River is intoxicating. There the sunshine is kind, the air is fragrant, and the sky is pierce-your-heart blue. In every direction the landscape is lush with mossy rocks, pine trees, and wild blueberries. The soft water of the river sparkles. Lime-green frogs sunbathe on a sandy beach, and loons sing their anthem of blues. Along the shore you hear the soothing sound of lapping water. And sometimes a balmy breeze ruffles the leaves of birch trees so they sound like nature's applause.

Blue-green days affect everyone who encounters them. They bring about a pleasant mood. Food tastes especially good; coffee, never better. After a day of swimming, my hair feels incredibly silky. Faces have a pink, sun-kissed glow. Some of us lie on the dock for hours just to be rocked by gentle waves, while others look for shells or skip rocks down by Myrtle's Beach. Here on the river, life's frenetic pace slows down to the beat of a resting heart.

Years ago my grandparents Raymond and Myrtle were naturally attracted to the land of blue-green days. In the early years of their marriage, they hopped on a train heading north from Toronto with their tent, some dried goods, and a canoe. In those days, you told the conductor where you wanted to get off and the engineer stopped the train. After the ride, the couple paddled into the region known as Algonquin Park to explore and camp.

Raymond found a location with four trees that were equal in size and distance from each other, like four posts of a large bed. He cut the trees down, leaving the stumps several feet high. Splitting the trunks, he used the rough planks to build a crude platform on top of the stumps. Together, they piled dried grasses on top to make a mattress. Myrtle covered the grasses with canvas and bedding while Raymond hung a hand-sewn tent over the bed, tying its corners to other trees. Then, if the rains came, their camp bed would be dry.

My grandparents lived in the woods for a month during their summers, eating small-mouthed bass and blueberries, along with their dried goods. When necessary, they canoed to a trading post for more supplies. They relished a simple life of watching birds, fishing, and swimming. They loved the north woods of Ontario so much, they built a cabin on the French River less than a hundred miles from where they originally camped.

With help from a local man over several summers, my grandfather constructed a log cabin. They finished the stone fireplace in 1938. My mother can remember carrying water up from the river. I even remember Old John, the creepy outhouse, and the giant spiders that took up residence there. Later on, two more cabins were built, and today the camp continues as the setting for blue-green days.

While we vacationed at the cabin almost every summer, our time there wasn't only about vacation, or even nature, as pristine as it was. For me, summers on the river were a point of contact with God. My grandmother felt a spiritual longing for the same and wrote a creed in the form of a little poem. She typed it, placed it on a little piece of wood, and framed the edges with birch bark. The creed still sits on the mantle over the stone fireplace in the original cabin.

> Here is a place to rest, a time for relaxation.
> Here Nature's at her best, releasing you from frustration.
>
> Here's a place for laughter, a place where friend meets friend.
> Discord must not enter, nor wills be made to bend.
>
> Here God's love surrounds us. Let's listen to His will.
> Not always in loud voices, but by sometimes being still.

Her poem captured me. My knowledge of God and feelings for him intensified in these three little cabins, tucked away in a green forest along a shining blue river. At home I was distracted with the busyness of school and friends. When we left for the cabin, life changed. Down by the water or on walks through the woods, there was time to daydream about God.

One summer at the cabin when I was nine, Nancy and I thought it would be fun to have a church service and invite our closest neighbors. My sister was a big organizer. She decided that we should be the ministers, if you can imagine clergy with pigtails. What we lacked in qualifications, we made up for in enthusiasm.

Using an assortment of chairs, we formed rows with a center aisle (in case someone wanted to get married later). Using an old washstand for an altar, we covered it with a white tablecloth, decorated with freshly picked ferns and a small wooden cross. Everything was ready, and best of all—it was a blue-green day.

As our parishioners arrived from the cabin next door, it suddenly occurred to me we didn't have a sermon. Somehow we had forgotten that part. I panicked, feeling the stage fright that gripped me at my piano recitals. *Dad. Surely he could come up with something on short notice.*

I saw him trudging up the stone steps toward me, his Bible under his arm. Grabbing his hand, I explained my dilemma and hurried him along. We sat on the steps of a wooden footbridge, and he leafed through his Bible. He knew right where to look. Quietly, he read me Jesus's parable of the sower,[1] explaining the symbolism with words I understood.

I pictured the sower with his bag of seeds, tossing them here and there along the road. How frustrated he must have felt when the birds came and ate them. Probably those annoying black crows. I imagined him waving his arms, chasing the birds away to no avail.

Then he scattered seeds in rocky soil, but without moisture, they didn't grow. The air must have been hot and dry. Some seeds grew among the thorns, but sadly, the brambles choked them out.

Yet the seeds he sowed on the good soil took root, and the crop grew a hundred times as great. I envisioned the sower surrounded by scores of baskets full of fruit, wearing a great big smile on his face. Vivid images filled my mind as Dad read.

Jesus explains how the seed is the word of God and the soil represents the condition of people's hearts. Regretfully, Dad said, some people resist God. Others are shallow in their faith, only believing for a short time. Still others are enthusiastic about God and even grow a little, but they eventually get distracted by the worries, riches, and pleasures of the world. Even so, some will hear God's words with an honest and good heart and grow into maturity.

I was nine, and I got it. The parable was like a puzzle we had to figure out. Of course, Jesus gave significant clues. But even as a child I understood that God spoke metaphorically (although *metaphor* was not yet a term in my vocabulary). In essence, God uses things in the natural world as symbols that point to spiritual truths.

By now our congregation was seated, and thankfully, I'd found a sermon. The audience seemed unusually attentive. We skipped the offering and ended with a song and a prayer, but the parable remained in my thoughts long afterward. In fact, it stayed with me for years. I wanted to be that good soil, ready to receive God's seeds.

God is a storyteller. As a child, this appealed to me. The symbolic pictures, metaphors, and parables throughout the Bible fascinated me. It was already my language, because I grew up with stories like *The Tortoise and the Hare, The Princess and the Pea,* and *The Little Engine That Could.* I understood those childhood tales were not real. They illustrated a truth, explaining intangible ideas in a concrete way.

In my early teens, I concocted my own symbolic ways to understand spiritual things. For example, the mystery of the Trinity made sense to me if I used an analogy from basic chemistry: God is our foundation, solid like ice. Jesus was God as a man, and like water, took the shape of its container. The Holy Spirit, though hard to see, goes everywhere like steam. They were all the same in substance, but different in form.

I think in this parallel fashion as I read the Bible. Even though the text is ancient, if you have ears to hear, the message is current. For instance, in college I studied the Old Testament story of Exodus. As I read the narrative, the Holy Spirit unlocked the meaning to me. Suddenly the text seemed highly symbolic of the Christian life.

The Jews were slaves in Egypt. God called Moses to rescue them, but it was no small task. A struggle ensued, and they encountered fierce opposition to their freedom. But God supported Moses with supernatural power and miracles, and once freed, the Israelites headed toward the Promised Land. But it was not theirs yet. Getting there involved a deadly wilderness, which was no field trip, and multiple tests and trials revealed what was in their hearts. They were ready to go back to Egypt simply to have food. They became their worst selves. But God's chosen were in the University of Character Development, and along the way some learned to depend on God. They pressed on toward the goal, because the Promised Land was real, and the journey was not endless.

The story is a profile of the Christian life, down to the last detail: bondage, freedom, a difficult journey, doubts, rebellion, growth, and the promise of a new tomorrow. We are the spiritual Israelites of today.

God continued to reveal truths as I learned the metaphorical language of the Bible. In my childhood, he gave me a measure of spiritual understanding with a simple story of a man planting some seeds. Every time I reread the story, it portrayed the same clear picture: God was looking for people who were ready to receive his truth.

As I matured, I believed the parable was about evangelism. Like the sower, we go out into the world with God's message of forgiveness and heaven, hoping to find people with open hearts.

But then I received a new thought about the same parable from author Stephen Strang.[2] He noted that the sower parable could have a larger meaning beyond evangelism. According to Jesus, if the seeds represent the Word of God, this parable could also be about learning to hear God's *fresh* voice. Twice in the same chapter, Jesus says, If anyone "has ears to hear, let him hear."[3] How odd. Jesus said this phrase before and after the sower parable, framing the story with his point. Hearing God is in present tense, meaning right now. It's supposed to be an ongoing experience in the Christian life.

If so, an interpretation of the parable would go something like this: Some Christians don't believe direct contact with God is possible. They know God spoke in a historical way through the Bible but turn a deaf ear to hearing God today. This theological position is safe even though the Bible gives ample evidence otherwise. Will God's seeds go unnoticed and be eaten by the birds?

Others attend church and like the idea that their faith is a relationship, not a religion. It sounds like a great idea and all—communicating with God. But they don't give it much thought. They occasionally pray to God, but aren't expecting any reply in return. Consequently, their seeds may never grow. Their roots are shallow, and their soil is just too rocky.

Other people believe God is speaking today, and they want to experience his voice, but life is incredibly busy. Their cell phones are constantly sounding off while they dash from business meetings to the gym and on to dinner and a movie. After church, there's laundry to do and a football game on TV. Easily distracted, they fail to notice God left a few words on their voice mail or a text message. Will thorns choke out their seeds?

But for those who believe contact with God is possible—those who pause, take a second look, and get quiet enough to listen—God will speak. As a result, a deeper relationship with him can take root and grow, making their lives fruitful.

A parable is a concise image with a larger meaning. When Jesus told parables, he was handing out puzzle pieces. This particular parable became a significant piece of a larger puzzle, forming a picture of God's desire to communicate with me. Suddenly it shifted into focus.

When my father calls me from Canada and tells me it's a blue-green day, he's using a code phrase for so much more. In my family, that phrase's connotation is full of images, colors, smells, and sounds, rich with our own personal history.

In the same way, when my heavenly Father calls to me, I usually know what he's saying, but sometimes I have some decoding to do.

I'll give you an example.

One morning God highlighted a particular verse about his undying love: Song of Solomon 7:10 says, "I am my beloved's, and his desire is for me." These ten simple words, spoken by a bride certain of her husband's love, had a life-giving effect on me. Rejection has been a theme in my life, as it is in many lives. I have experienced betrayal, hatred, and persecution from others. There have been seasons of estrangement and alienation with friends and family. I have known loneliness. It's not an overstatement to say that human relationships are predictably disappointing.

But God's love is consistent, and he began using this verse to communicate his love to me. He wants me to say unequivocally, "I am God's beloved and his desire is for me." As the "bride of Christ," I am valued and cherished by him even when human relationships break down.

Now it's one thing to read a verse and feel God's love wrap around you for a moment. Maybe even for a day. But it doesn't have to stop there. If you memorize a verse, it provides more possibilities for communication. Song of Solomon 7:10 became a code phrase between God and me, and he brought it up repeatedly in uncanny ways, with perfect timing.

One day I was depressed, though I can't remember why. As I drove down Main Street, I noticed that a movie started at 7:10 p.m. Hmm. I remembered the verse: "I am my beloved's, and his desire is for me."

Another day I was having a difficult time with our teenagers. (I know that's hard to believe.) I stopped at a convenience store for some after-school snacks. At the counter I found myself stupefied: our refreshments totaled $7.10, but I was refreshed in a much greater way. This seemed to occur with increasing frequency, although I did not look for the numbers or expect them to appear.

When God has something important to say, he will find a way to say it again and again. Many times the license plate on the car in front of me ended with the numbers 710. I cannot explain this. I was at a friend's house in Seattle one night when the power went off. Her digital clock flashed 7:10. Another evening I was watching TV and a cell phone commercial came on. The phone wiggled like it was ringing, and a voice said, "The message is for you!" The model number on the phone was 710.

Then one morning, God really unraveled me. Duncan and I have two coffee makers, because we like our joe just so (yes, we're coffee snobs). I came into the kitchen to make my morning cup and saw that the clocks on the two coffee makers showed different times. Both were wrong, but I didn't want to bother resetting them. As I stirred milk into my cup, I noticed my husband's coffee maker read 7:10, though it was actually about 8:15.

I smiled. *Hi God. I love you too.*

When I came back for my second cup around 9:00, *my* coffee maker's clock now showed the time as 7:10. There was no earthly reason why my clock should be showing that number.

I sank down on one knee. Sometimes you just can't stand up during a supernatural moment. It had been a tough week, and I felt out of sorts and weary. With my arms resting on the kitchen counter and my head bowed low, I worshiped this God who knows me so well. My chest heaved with deep sighs as I drank in his presence. *Oh God, you really love me. You really do.*

Of course, we know it's not about the numbers. It's about a connection and the knowledge that God is bigger than our waking reality. He holds it all in his hand, and he offers it to us that we might see it, touch it, taste it, and experience the joy of his nearness.

Every day the Holy Spirit is sowing God's words for those who can understand them. Whether his words bring salvation or develop relationship with him is not worth fighting over. Both matter. He is looking for the good soil of an open heart and a listening ear. When he says something to you, it will be in your own language, significant in a personal and specific kind of way.

It will be exactly what you need to hear. All you have to do is listen.

ELEVEN

Thanksgiving.com
A Door Called Gratitude

*"And My people shall be
satisfied with My goodness,"
declares the Lord.*
—JEREMIAH 31:14

One evening, I sank into an easy chair after dinner. Leaning back, I rested my head, exhaling a deep breath. My heart was heavy with discouragement. Earlier days of trauma left residual fallout on our girls and our marriage. Healing and change were not won overnight. In fact, recovery was a long, slow journey. A person's heart can get weary along the way.

As I closed my eyes, a Web address appeared on the screen of my mind. In clear letters I saw www.thanksgiving.com. *How random,* I thought. It was a hot summer night, months away from Turkey Day.

An idea flashed through my head. What if God was the source of that peculiar impression? If so, maybe he had something to say. I knew that sometimes an interruption of my thoughts could be a stirring of the Holy Spirit. But like I said, I don't always pay attention. This time, my scattered mind slowed down. *What are you saying to me, Lord?*

I waited. I waited longer. It seemed as if God delayed his response until he had my full attention. Then he spoke. *Visit me.*

I didn't hear anything audible. Yet the impression was distinct. The words came like a simple invitation.

If God speaks in all languages across every culture, he must also speak across time in contemporary symbols and images. My curiosity came alive. *Let's see,* I thought. *To visit that "Web site," the keyword might be gratitude.* Perhaps God wanted me to acknowledge what was good in my life. I knew gratitude was a good antidote to discouragement.

Okay, I get it.

Of course, our cabin in the north woods of Ontario came up immediately. I felt very grateful for that. As life's complexities accelerated with each passing year, the cabin remained the place where our family reverted to Little-House-on-the-Prairie simplicity. Time was the gift: time to pick wild blueberries and savor them…time to dangle our feet in the cool water of the river.

For many years at the cabin, we didn't have TV, movies, cell phones, or computers. We didn't even have a land line. Taking a break from the hectic pace of life was intentional. We also took a hiatus from the daily fare of too much catastrophic news.

Some people in our sound-bite, fast-moving, action-packed-movie existence might think a retreat to a cabin in the woods quite dull. But it rarely felt that way to me. Entertainment just came in different forms. The excitement for the day might have been a large bug with long spindly antennas flying around the kitchen. One evening a bat flew down the chimney. Imagine the screaming women. A few summers ago, we arrived to find a beaver building his dam under our dock. Our neighbor told us to leave a radio playing down by the water because apparently beavers hate country music.

Then there was the summer that Simon, a twenty-something friend from London, came for a visit. He slept alone in the oldest cabin in the bedroom by the kitchen. As fate would have it, he also slept in the nude.

One moonless night, he heard the screen door open, then the cupboard. He thought someone was getting a late-night snack. Soon the sound of bare feet shuffled toward his door. In the pitch darkness, he wondered who was entering his room and grew a little more concerned. He didn't dare move. Suddenly, a cold hand touched the middle of his chest. Naked or not, he exploded from his covers and flew through the back door.

Outside in the damp night air, he remembered his wet bathing trunks hung on the clothesline. As Simon wriggled into his clammy suit, hopping around on one foot, my husband heard the commotion and stumbled upon the scene. Broomstick in hand, Duncan tiptoed into the old cabin through the back door with Simon close behind. When he flipped on the lights, they startled a giant raccoon that immediately bolted out the kitchen door. The red screen door slammed shut, echoing in the still night. With the crisis abated, Simon cautiously returned to bed, but his adrenaline was still peaking. I don't think he'll soon forget the small cold hand.

Dull? Not a chance. Now gratitude was flowing.

Another memory came. Then another. Memories surged into my mind. I thought of my Gram, an elegant woman who welcomed the mayhem of seven grandchildren. Once she baked five—count 'em—*five* different pies for us: apple, cherry, blueberry, peach, and raisin.

On her living room coffee table sat a silver dish with an ornate lid; it was stocked full of gumdrops. All the grandchildren were giddily aware of the stash, but we were quite sure our parents didn't know. Gram never said a word, and kept it regularly stocked.

At night, Nancy and I slipped into beds of pressed cotton sheets and soft blankets. Gram tickled our arms and sang, "I Wish I Was a Monkey in the Zoo." Whenever I lost a baby tooth, the tooth fairy would come and leave pennies, nickels, and dimes under the corners of her area rugs. She taught me how to make peanut brittle, stretching it lacy thin with hot buttery fingers on a marble slab. Her basement held a treasure trove of artifacts, including a huge doll house, a book about Paris, two Civil War swords, and an old-fashioned washing machine with rollers.

In my junior-high years, she invited her granddaughters to a "house party." Today, they're called sleepovers. She served cokes and pretzels to us while we watched old black-and-white movies. That weekend my cousin sat on Gram's glass-top table, and it suddenly shattered. A huge shard fell, slicing the skin above my ankle bone. A doctor stitched up the laceration, but after the local anesthetic wore off, pain descended like a dropped piano. In a pre-Vicodin world, my foot throbbed unbearably, but Gram stayed up half the night with me trying to alleviate my suffering with ice packs, pillows, and a few aspirins.

During my college years, I would drive the hour-or-so distance to visit her. At night we'd lie side by side in twin beds moved together, so she could read her grandfather's journal out loud to me. His words recounted a fascinating story of a journey to the Holy Land by ship. I discovered a strong connection with Gram and my ancestors who held a deep passion for God. In the morning, she set a breakfast table fit for a queen.

As I grew into adulthood, signs of her decline became evident. One morning at breakfast, she leaned forward and said in a hushed voice, "If I die tomorrow, don't be sad. I've had a very good life, and I feel the everlasting arms of God around me." I nodded, speechless, as tears pooled in my eyes. She felt secure with God and imparted this to me in measure.

Good-byes at her back door became increasingly difficult. I hugged and kissed her as if it might be the last time. We would wave and hide our sorrow. Then one ordinary day, she quietly slipped away. God comforted me with the psalmist's words saying: "Precious in the sight of the LORD is the death of His godly ones."[1] I missed her so much…and still do. Life with Gram will remain a story about fun, sugar, and love—and the greatest of these was love.

More scenes popped up in my mind, and soon I was fully engaged as I searched through my life history. I had so much to be thankful for, and I wrote it down, day after day. Yet as I focused on my adult life, finding gratitude in the present proved much harder.

One evening while watching the movie *Hope Floats,* God opened an intense pocket of sorrow. A small-town beauty queen named Birdee Pruitt finds her seemingly charmed life ruined when her husband admits to having an affair with her best friend. Life hands her the jilted housewife part. Birdee returns to her hometown, embarrassed and brokenhearted. Locals seem to enjoy rubbing it in, but she is shattered.

It wasn't the affair itself that gripped me in the story. It was how long it took her to get over it. We live in a time when adultery is commonplace. People divorce quickly and life goes on. In the movie, Birdee's despair isn't centered on the loss of her husband, who seems shallow and self-absorbed. But rather that life turned out so different than she thought it would.[2]

Many people have suffered far worse tragedies. There are daily tyrannies of abuse, poverty, neglect, and rejection. In many ways, life in America is vastly easier when you think globally.

But I resonated with Birdee's deep disappointment. Life was different from what I thought it would be. Some hopeful, innocent part of me had collapsed, and I had left myself for dead. Like tangled coat hangers, I felt caught in the tenacious grip of negativity. God's request for me to work on being thankful was timely.

During this time I met a little girl named Milaina. She had been abandoned at birth by her single mother and lived in an Albanian orphanage. Caregivers mistakenly thought she had a dislocated hip and kept her in a crib for years. The misdiagnosis and lack of treatment ruined her hip, not to mention her physical development. She was bottle fed for the first five years and didn't know how to eat solid food or even speak. Who would adopt an eight-year-old with that many problems?

Enter Nell and Ron. They had already raised three children of their own, yet after stacks of paperwork, long waiting periods, and great expense, Milaina became their daughter. Specialists said she probably wouldn't talk, walk, or bond with anyone because of her institutional isolation, but Nell and Ron seemed undaunted.

Later, I saw Nell at a picnic, and I asked her about Milaina. As we talked, Milaina came over to grab her mother's hand and lean against her. After several surgeries, she can walk quite well. She communicates with sign language and is obviously attached to her parents.

Nell told me they were working on socialization and had approached our local Wal-Mart to help. The store manager, eager to assist, explained "the Milaina project" to all the employees. When Milaina enters the store, an announcement booms over the sound system: "Attention all associates, Milaina is in the store." She receives a balloon at the customer service desk so employees will recognize her. They make an effort to greet her or have a short dialogue. One Wal-Mart supervisor, Concetta, took a special interest in Milaina, extending warmth and kindness far beyond her job description. Nell's words broke up with emotion as she recounted the story.[3]

In her view, there was so much to be thankful for.

I felt acutely humbled. I had enjoyed every blessing in childhood and grew up to find that life was not as pretty and nice as I thought. Milaina was robbed of every childhood blessing but was given a life much better than she could have imagined. Both our experiences were painful in different ways, but I was stuck in discouragement. I still needed to break free.

Even small amounts of self-pity are dangerous to the soul. Negativity is an ugly cell where every inmate is both prisoner and warden. But gratitude is the way to freedom.

Another night, God spoke through the psalms with such precision, it was as though he pulled up a chair next to me:

> Reproach has broken my heart and I am so sick...I am afflicted
> and in pain...[Yet] I will praise the name of God with song and
> magnify Him with *thanksgiving*. And it will please the LORD better

than an ox or a young bull with horns and hoofs. The humble
have seen it and are glad; you who seek God, *let your heart revive.*[4]

I closed my Bible and my eyes as I thought about the last four words.
It doesn't matter if you're rich, poor, American, or Albanian. It doesn't
matter if you're male or female. You can be very young or very old or
somewhere in between. Pain is tantamount to being human. The real
danger, though, is losing your heart along the way.

God invited me to visit him through the door of gratitude, calling
my heart back to life. And he didn't let up on it either. Apparently this
was imperative for me to understand.

One night at the Salvation Army Church downtown, a group of
friends held a two-hour service of singing and Scripture reading. I
decided to go. Lying on the church bench in the back row, I felt weighed
down with weariness. Were all my efforts just a religious exercise, a
contrived effort to whip up an "attitude of gratitude"? Had I only been
coasting on childhood memories, ignoring the difficulties of the present?
I felt sorely tested as a mother and a wife. Covering my eyes with my
arm, I wanted to turn off my mind. But persistent thoughts intruded
like telemarketers. Too tired to sing, I listened.

Song after song, piano sounds filled the room with beautiful
melodies. I began to breathe in deeply, peacefully. Scriptures were read out
loud, and they filled my mind with thoughts and images. My entire body
began to unwind. Though I wasn't participating, I was still benefiting.

Throughout the first hour of worship, I kept hoping they would
play the well-known hymn, "Holy, Holy, Holy." To my surprise, the
lyrics went up on the overhead. Was it coincidence? Maybe. Or maybe
God heard my thoughts. I abruptly rose up and joined in, singing from
the tips of my toes.

And as I did, the doors of my heart flung wide open.

In that moment, God's presence descended on me with a tangible
glory. I experienced it like a spring downpour of life-giving rain on parched

ground, turning everything dull into vibrant colors. I took a deep breath and tension released from the muscles around my eyes.

When the song ended, I couldn't move. I didn't want him to go away. So I lingered, sensing a spiritual sneeze moment in the making. A stream of thoughts entered my mind. God reminded me of his provision during distressing times. I pictured the rabbit he sent on that New Hampshire road, and my lost diamond in the garden that, against all odds, he'd returned to me. Specific verses came back to mind. God had turned them into promises for my life. The still, small voice of the Holy Spirit spoke in a continual flow of images, scriptures, and memories, overcoming my anxious thoughts. Jesus said this would happen. His Spirit brings things to our remembrance.[5]

His love streamed down, eclipsing my gratitude for earthly things and filling me with love for him alone. I sent my thanks back to God, my heart pounding within. The music continued, and I worshiped from deep inside, a worship unlike any other religious activity I've ever experienced.

Since that night, I realized praising God in the best of times is nothing compared to praising him in the worst of times. To find gratitude for God in times of personal disappointment, or even hopelessness, is a way of saying, "I trust you no matter what it looks like down here." In any language, that spells faith, and faith is what moves the heart of God.

C. S. Lewis once said, "It is in the process of being worshipped that God communicates His presence to men. It is not of course the only way. But for many people at many times the 'fair beauty of the Lord' is revealed chiefly or only while they worship Him together."[6]

We can be with God, connected through time and space in an instant. We enter his presence and pass through his gates when we have thanksgiving in our hearts.[7]

TWELVE

Unwinding

Off the Treadmill and into the Adventure

We can't have full knowledge all at once.
We must start by believing; then afterwards we may be led
on to master the evidence for ourselves.

—Saint Thomas Aquinas

t was Wednesday evening. Our home group had just ended. I stood in the kitchen rinsing coffee cups when Peter approached me, his brow twisted with concern.

"Your chair. It was so close to the edge of the step."

I paused, fully expecting him to continue. When he didn't, I said, "Oh. I didn't know." I scanned his face looking for clues. He gathered his thoughts.

"You could have easily fallen off. I tried to ignore it, but I was gripped by the thought. Something about it…" He scanned the floor, and then looked back at me.

"Really. And why are you telling me now?"

"I sensed God was saying something, well, symbolically…you understand."

"I'm not sure." I sensed a sneeze moment was brewing.

Peter searched for the right words to interpret his message. "Something concerning your life is near an edge or has reached a limit of some sort, and you're in danger." His words were bold, but his demeanor remained humble and kind. "Does this make any sense?"

Something in me clicked.

"Yeah. I think so. I've pushed my life to the edge of exhaustion, and I guess you could say I'm in danger." At the time, I was in full bustle mode at the peak of Marthahood, and God had given me the exact same warning on two other occasions in different ways. Peter was his third messenger.

The first warning came when I read *Oswald Chambers: Abandoned to God,* David McCasland's biography of the author of *My Utmost for His Highest,* the most popular Christian devotional of all time. Chambers was sold out for God and truly lived the title of his now-famous devotional. Sadly he died at the age of forty-three. What got my attention was the fact that he died on my birthday, and I was about to turn forty-three in a matter of days. A coincidence? Maybe, maybe not. I sat upright, seriously engaged in the story now.

Chambers was serving as a chaplain in World War I when he suffered an acute appendicitis attack, which led to an emergency appendectomy. The surgery went well, perfectly normal in all ways. But in the days following, his body failed to recover because of fatigue.

Family and friends asked many questions. "Why had he waited so long to seek treatment? Why hadn't someone recognized the symptoms of appendicitis earlier and insisted he get help? Why had he worked so long without rest, depleting his physical reserve to almost nothing?"[1]

Forty-three, exhausted…dead.

The message was astonishingly clear. It even took my breath away, but I didn't slow down much. My overdoing had become a deep-seated way of life. Yes, I was more aware of it, but how do you stop a runaway truck with worn-down brakes?

A second warning came in a dream. For ten mornings one summer, I set apart some extended time to worship and pray. The early hours seemed like my best shot at uninterrupted time. The alarm clock beeped relentlessly each day, and a steaming cup of coffee helped me keep the commitment. I grabbed some CDs and my Bible and trudged up the hill to the little barn behind our house.

The first morning I worshiped God with music. I prayed for everything I could think of. Eventually, I ran out of things to say. In time I became quieter and listened more, sometimes with music playing, sometimes in silence. On the tenth morning, I lay down to pray and unintentionally fell asleep.

But God still spoke.

Indeed God speaks…in a dream, a vision of the night, when
sound sleep falls on men, while they slumber in their beds,
then He opens the ears of men, and seals their instruction,
that He may turn man aside from his conduct, and keep man
from pride.[2]

In the dream, I'm sitting cross-legged on the floor while Jesus strolls around the circumference of the room. He tells me he's made a major decision: my hands need to be amputated at my forearms. He doesn't seem upset about it, and he looks at me with a Mona Lisa smile.

"You'll get it," he whispers, like he's sharing a great secret.

Shocked and distressed, I argue. "What? You can't be serious! I'm a mom, and I need to drive—and cook— and write checks!" He walks on in silence, his hands clasped behind his back. "This is a huge mistake! People depend on me!"

He nods, unruffled by my protests.

"You'll get it."

"This can't happen to me! I can't believe this is okay with you! It doesn't make any sense. Please listen to…"

I look down and my hands are already gone. It's over. I'm in a state of shock as liquid streams from my arms. In a matter of seconds, I will probably bleed to death. Slumping back against the wall, I feel stung by the harshness of his verdict. Seconds turn into minutes, yet I don't lose consciousness. Looking down at my stubbed limbs, it occurs to me that the fluid flowing out of my arms isn't blood but water.

"You'll get it," echoed in my mind as I woke up. I immediately checked my arms. The dream seemed so real. *God, what was that about?* A clear phrase invaded my thoughts.

We must stop all your doing.

Doing, doing, doing. Yep, that was me. Going, going, going. The message was pointed, but he spoke without condemnation or even a hint of disappointment. Then his written Word confirmed the fresh word he had spoken through my dream:

> If your right hand makes you stumble, cut it off and throw it
> from you; for it is better for you to lose one of the parts of your
> body, than for your whole body to go into hell.[3]

Although the verse spoke of hell, I knew my eternal relationship with God wasn't in jeopardy. He was, however, emphatically declaring that my "doing" set a harmful pattern for my life and wasn't what he wanted from me anyway.

I remember reading in *Uncle Tom's Cabin* about Eliza's desperate flight when her four-year-old son was about to be sold into slavery. She takes her son and flees with supernatural endurance, walking for miles, not eating or sleeping. Finally, she crosses the Ohio River on big chunks of ice with bleeding feet. At any moment they could have slipped into the icy water, perishing together in the cold. The author, Harriet Beecher Stowe, comments about Eliza's endurance:

> Sublime is the dominion of the mind over the body, that, for a
> time, can make flesh and nerve impregnable, and string the
> sinews like steel, so that the weak become so mighty.[4]

After reading Stowe's words, I wrote in my journal how Eliza's visceral determination was similar to the Martha Syndrome in me. Eliza's persistence was noble. However, the same resolute willpower in my world was destructive. I was doing the Christian life in my own stubborn strength.

I'm not sure we quite understand what trusting God really means. What will it take to get through to us? There's a lot of Christian busyness that detracts or even runs counter to what God is doing. Like the Grand Inquisitor in Dostoevsky's novel, I had my own big ideas about fixing the world. But I missed the greater plans God has for his creation.

Scripture is clear about this. Solomon warned: "do not lean on your own understanding."[5] The psalmist wrote that unless the Lord builds the house, we labor in vain.[6] Jesus said that without him, we can do nothing.[7] Paul spoke forcefully about speculations, pretensions, and lofty ideas raised up against the knowledge of God. He called them strongholds that need to be demolished.[8]

But I was driven by another scripture. James wrote, "What use is it, my brethren, if someone says he has faith but he has no works? Can that faith save him?…faith without works is useless…I will show you my faith *by* my works."[9] Barbed like a porcupine quill, this passage needled its way under the skin of my faith, producing a works-based approach to life. God rescued me from my warped thinking with a solemn warning spoken in three distinct ways. "We must stop all your *doing.*"

God took me to a new place in Scripture one morning. Now it's one of my favorite stories. You'll find it in the last chapter of John. The crisis of Jesus's crucifixion is over and many of the disciples have lost heart. Peter decides to go fishing and takes a bunch of the guys with him. They fish all night and catch absolutely nothing. Not a single fish.

When dawn breaks, a man on the beach calls to them. "Catch anything?"

They answer. "No." It's been a tough week all around.

The man yells back, "Try the other side of the boat. You'll find a catch."

Now how would you feel if you'd been fishing all night and some stranger comes up and tells you how to do your job? They are probably exasperated, but they throw the net anyway. To their surprise, the catch is so huge they can't pull it in.

John looks at Peter and makes an almost unthinkable speculation, "It is the Lord."[10]

Jesus stood on the beach of my world too, calling out, "Throw your net *where I say.* You'll find a catch." But I didn't get it at first. I threw my net of good intentions on every side of life, pulling in feeble results. My determination led me nowhere. Ironically, Oswald Chambers summed up the point God was making. Later, I read it with new understanding:

> The snare in Christian work is to rejoice in successful service, to rejoice in the fact that God has used you. [But this is entirely the wrong mind-set. Instead…] Keep your relationship right with Him, then whatever circumstances you are in, and whoever you meet day by day, *He is pouring rivers of living water through you,* and it is of His mercy that He does not let you know it…*It is the work that God does through us that counts, not what we do for Him.*[11]

I reread the last sentence several times. It's not about what I do for God. The amputation dream depicted the end of my "doing." Only then could God's living water flow through me to others. It's all about what God's up to. And sometimes he involves me.

In his book *Memoirs of Childhood and Youth,* Albert Schweitzer echoed Chambers on this point when he wrote:

> So many people gave me something or were something to me without knowing it.… If we had before us those who have thus been a blessing to us, and could tell them how it came about,

they would be amazed to learn what passed over from their life into ours. Similarly, not one of us knows what effect his life produces, and what he gives to others; that is hidden from us and must remain so.[12]

I, on the other hand, kept score with my list of spiritual merit badges. When in doubt, I served at church, volunteered at my children's schools, worked on various committees, and joined assorted small groups. But what if God was saying, "Did I ask you to accomplish all those things?" There are many good things to do. There will *always* be many good things to do. In the meantime, I needed to stop and explore God's agenda. What did he want to do through me? I had to reverse the entire thing.

As C. S. Lewis said in *Mere Christianity*, a new kind of faith arises after a person has tried his level best and comes up short. In other words, we realize a deeper faith when we find "our bankruptcy" before God. Lewis maintained that we cannot go on with God until we have discovered this fact.[13] As my own bankruptcy became clear, my approach to life gradually turned like a giant, slow-moving ship. God was charting a new course.

I quit various commitments, relinquished my agenda, and the roar of life slowed down. I notice things when life is slower. It's easier to love people. It was also easier to hear God.

Hearing God's voice also involved a shift in my perspective. Instead of my to-do list, I began my day by asking God, "What are *you* doing today?" I found that powerful things happen in everyday moments when God says, "Throw your net here." I became more attentive, more in step with the Holy Spirit, sensing in the moment what God cared about in my little sphere of influence.

Soon, on an ordinary summer night, a pivotal experience reinforced the new direction God was leading me.

The phone rang. My neighbor Valerie said they wouldn't need Katie to baby-sit after all. Their tiny daughter, Lauren, was deathly ill: fever, diarrhea, and severe dehydration. They planned to fly her to Salt Lake City in the morning, as her condition was rapidly deteriorating. When I hung up, powerful words abruptly entered my mind like a flashing neon light.

Go pray for them.

My skin tingled all over. Like John said to Peter, I knew in my spirit, "It's the Lord." I didn't know the couple all that well and was uncertain of their spiritual leanings. Going to their home was a risk. I told Duncan the situation, and unlike me, he didn't hesitate. "Let's go!" Our daughter Sarah went along, and we walked up the gravel road to knock on their door.

Valerie answered. Pale and disheveled, she spoke in hushed tones. She was pregnant with their third child though she barely showed. The front hallway was dark and their dog hummed a low growl. She motioned us in, but was clearly confused about why we were there.

"We wondered if we could pray for the baby," Duncan said. She paused for a second, but agreed, and ushered us into the nursery. Lauren had just fallen asleep. Because of the fever, she slept in short fits, waking up every half hour. My heart ached for Valerie. I knew what it was like to stay up all night with a sick baby.

"Could I put my hand on her while we pray?" Duncan whispered. Valerie nodded. Duncan spoke a simple prayer of protection and asked God to heal her little girl. I turned to Valerie.

"Can I pray for you too?"

In the dim glow of the night-light, tears glistened on her cheeks. Again she nodded. "No one has ever prayed for me."

I asked God to calm her, give her his peace, and protect the baby in her womb. Afterward, I gave her a hug and felt her body slump into my arms, her weariness overruling decorum. We walked back down the road to our house.

The next day, Valerie's husband, Jerry, called. He had been in town getting medicine when we prayed for his family. His voice trembled with excitement.

"You won't believe this," he said.

"What happened?" I asked.

"I came home after you left. Since our daughter was sleeping, we went to bed ourselves. We were both exhausted. At 4 a.m., I woke up in a panic thinking Lauren had died. She had been waking up all hours of the night. But her little chest was moving up and down, and her fever was completely gone! Val and I climbed back into bed and talked about God for hours. This morning Lauren is awake, eating, playing, full of energy. She seems perfectly well!"

"Wow." I didn't know what else to say.

"There's no explanation other than God." The joy in his voice was unmistakable. I couldn't help but admit my own surprise. Chambers' words came to mind: "It is the work that God does through us that counts, not what we do for Him."

"Jerry, that's…amazing. I'm so glad."

"But you guys prayed and that made the difference."

Well, yes and no. God was ready to move like a giant ocean swell, rolling onto the shore, carrying his power, presence, and love into our neighbors' lives. And for reasons only he knows, we got to go along.

God was doing it. We just caught the wave.

When life was ripping at full speed, I missed God's promptings. I would have shrugged him off for the next committee meeting. Usually my mind was quick to rationalize a step of faith like this as intrusive, crazy, or unwelcome. I'd shrug it off or avoid it entirely.

But this time I didn't. Maybe I couldn't. Was God prodding me out of my safe house to stretch my understanding of his ways? I don't know. But I do know that I heard specific instructions, and they taught me something new, something completely opposite to the way I had been living my faith. What I strived to do in my own power was easy for the Holy Spirit. Now I was ready to watch God at work.

I've given up a make-it-happen approach to life. I'm ready to stop saving the world. My focus has changed. Stepping off the treadmill of constant busyness, exhaustion, and overcommitment, I'm looking for moments where I can say, "It's the Lord!" It's refreshing, it's adventure, but most of all, it's freedom.

Hmm. "Okay God, what are you up to today?"

THIRTEEN

Thoughts on Destiny
Made for a Purpose

How to make God laugh: Tell him your future plans.
—WOODY ALLEN

After the night God dropped in on our neighbors, I became convinced that a listening-to-God approach in everyday life embodied the essence of John 15. In that chapter Jesus talked about the vine and the branches working in simpatico.[1] To my surprise, that metaphor from nature became the seminal image of how God works through his followers, and it eventually freed me from the Martha Syndrome.

God was unwinding me, unraveling the "earn-this" mentality. In addition, my something-must-be-done vow had lost its drive. I was now convinced that I should only go fishing when Jesus told me where to throw the net. A critical shift was taking place in my spirituality.

I let go of many religious obligations, clearing the underbrush of old, dead habits. The pruning stimulated growth in my relationship with God. In the gospels God pointed out to me that Jesus resisted overactivity and often left the crowd to be alone with God. He didn't set up committees, task forces, and focus groups, but said that he only did what the Father was doing.[2] He watched, waited, and discerned God's plans for the day in the moment. His purposes were intentional, but his sensitivity to the Spirit remained in the here and now. This became my model.

In time, my goals became amazingly simple: Spend time with God to develop intimacy. Listen for his signals. Invite God into my day and allow him to rearrange my schedule. And finally, ask God to bring people to me who needed prayer. Living this way brought incredible liberty and inherently smacked of adventure. Every day was less regimented and more spontaneous and dynamic.

Unless you've worked for at least a year on a committee that required countless hours on tedious and relatively unimportant matters, you can't imagine how refreshing this felt. In retrospect, I wondered why I had wasted so much time. I cared about people, but some of those committee meetings seemed like a sideshow. Years ago my young daughter took a phone message for me, leaving a note on the counter: "Comedy Meeting, 7:00 on Tuesday." She meant committee. My father once said that some committees are like a bus with ten steering wheels. It's pretty tough to get anywhere. You probably know the feeling.

I laughed then, but now the thought of my old life makes my chest tighten. It's *so* not about what I did or thought I could do. My perspective was altered forever. God was the one moving throughout the earth, and at times, he invited me to go along for the ride.

Part of that change in awareness involved surrender. I had to yield my opinions, agendas, and timetables about how God should fix a broken world. I resisted the tendency to put him on trial concerning things I didn't understand. It sounds ridiculous, but it shows the hidden arrogance of my fix-it-all mind.

Trust didn't come easily.

The inner conflict of surrender reminded me of the struggle in giving birth. A smooth delivery involves trusting in a process that feels out of control. Tensing up interferes with the natural birth of a baby. In my case, when it came time to push and deliver my firstborn, I held back with all my might. The nurses finally convinced me I wouldn't split in two. If I trusted and participated with the urge to push, our baby would be born. Two pushes later, Katie arrived. A lot of women talk about the intensity of labor pains, but I remember the intense tug of war within me. Surrender was imperative.

Truly trusting God beyond Christianese platitudes is both a crisis of faith and a milestone of faith. Perhaps you've heard the saying: "Show me, God, and I'll believe." But God says, "Believe and I'll show you." It comes down to the all-important step of faith—to go as far as we know and take one more step. Life with God is far more exciting when you go beyond what you know or think you can explain.

So I embarked into new territory with God, believing it's the every-day, walking-with-Jesus kind of things that bring the kingdom of God to earth. Small responses to God that rarely make the nightly news—a prayer for a sick child, an act of kindness, the sacrifice in self-control, the work of forgiveness—these are the manifestations of faith.

But having said that, I also know that God creates each of us for a specific purpose. And often that purpose is inexplicably tied up with the desires of our hearts.

Take Vincent van Gogh. He felt certain he was called into ministry. For a season he pastored in Borinage, an impoverished Belgian mining district. He worked with the miners, shared their afflictions, and gave them almost all his earthly possessions. One winter, he donated his coat and wore only a shirt in freezing temperatures. He subsisted on a diet of bread and water. In the end, his religious efforts, though sincere, were deemed overzealous, and the Evangelical Committee did not renew his contract.

At the time, he called himself an idler and said, "Sometimes people in this position do not know themselves...yet they feel instinctively: I *am* capable of something, my existence *does* mean something!"[3] He turned to art and discovered the passion of his life. In his letters to his brother, Theo, he said he wanted his paintings to reflect what God is like. Indeed, "His art's ability to touch the hem of the Eternal derived from a profound and genuine longing for the sheltered security of religious faith."[4]

Oswald Chambers, in contrast, believed he was destined to be an artist. His schooling developed his natural abilities. In a letter he wrote, "Oh, if in the infinite goodness of God, He would permit me to be of use to His great cause in Art, then how could I contain such an honour; but His is the future not mine." So bent was he on pursuing art, he even said, "I shall never go into the ministry until God takes me by the scruff of the neck and throws me in."[5] But one day, a devout man told Chambers with conviction that his true calling was in ministry.

A battle ensued in Chambers' heart. He climbed to the highest hillside overlooking Edinburgh and spent the night waiting for confirmation from God. "As the hours wore on, his soul cried out in anguished silence. Sometime during the night, according to Chambers' account, he heard a voice that actually spoke these words, 'I want you in My service—but I can do without you.'"[6] That night he knew the course of his life would change. The path to ministry eventually unfolded, and he also found the passion of his life.

The spirit of God directed both men into their destinies. Otherwise we might have known them as a Dutch pastor and a Scottish artist, respectively. Nothing wrong with that. But it was not the calling God had planned for them.

The word *destiny* can cause some eye rolling in a Monty-Python-Holy-Quest kind of cynicism. But destiny is not mystical or corny. Destiny is about purpose, and according to Rick Warren, author of *The Purpose Driven Life,* the idea of purpose has ignited a fire under lukewarm Christianity throughout the world.

Destiny is not about being famous. It's not necessarily like a career you can identify and train for in college. It can be something you do that's different from how you make a living. For example, some of the best counselors in our town are hairdressers and emergency-room nurses. I know some skateboarders who "pastor" street kids.

Destiny is not inevitably something you do your whole life. You could spend most of your life in preparation, and finally, at the appointed time, your work is only for a short duration. Take Jesus, for example. Or how about Sir William Wallace from *Braveheart,* Joan of Arc, or Jim Elliot and his four friends who died as martyrs in Ecuador at the end of a spear? A person's destiny may be like one beautiful thread in an elaborate tapestry God is weaving, and sometimes the role the person played won't make any sense until he or she has eternal eyes. Think of John the Baptist.

Finding your destiny is by no means an easy road. You may find a purpose that feels like a fit. It must be God, you think. Finally you've found your yellow brick road, but the journey ahead won't be without challenges. A shrewd Enemy prowls around, hungry for victims. He vehemently doesn't want you to find the reason for which you were created.

The gospel version of the Christmas story tells how the Virgin Mary gave birth in a humble stable. The shepherds and wise men all come with their presents, and everyone is happy and glowing. But look at Revelation 12; the unseen spiritual forces surrounding Christ's birth paint quite a different drama:

> A great sign appeared in heaven: a woman clothed with the
> sun…and she was with child; and she cried out, being in labor
> and in pain to give birth. Then another sign appeared in heaven:
> and behold, a great red dragon…stood before the woman who
> was about to give birth, so that when she gave birth he might
> devour her child.[7]

The Enemy knew the destiny of Jesus's life and stood poised, ready to take him out. That's poles apart from the image of Jesus's idyllic years as a simple carpenter.

When God births in us the purpose for our lives, we face a level of spiritual warfare unlike anything we have ever known. With complicated deceptions and simple ones, the Enemy of our souls uses our own weaknesses to trip us up. It would be much easier to forget it and have a barbeque. It's far less complicated to be distracted or entertained. But if we accept that sort of mediocrity, we will miss our adventure.

I wouldn't say I failed to notice the destiny messages God sent my way, but I was slow on the uptake. Ever since junior high, I loved journaling. I collected quotes, wrote poems, and composed long letters to God. But in my early twenties, my cursive looked uneven and ugly as I addressed my wedding invitations. Twelve years later, I could barely address an envelope. Something was definitely wrong.

To my relief, my symptoms didn't indicate one of the scary diagnoses. Two different neurologists told me I had a known disorder called "writer's cramp." (At the time it wasn't funny, though now the term is a little joke between God and me.) When I would write, the minuscule muscles that coordinate the precise movements of my hand were prone to freezing up. The condition can ruin the career of a violinist, and sometimes it happens to the lip muscles of trumpet and trombone players. It's not from the overuse of certain muscles like carpal tunnel syndrome. In fact, doctors don't know why it happens. What they do know is there's no known case in which it improved. I could try to write with my left hand, but the same thing would likely happen. So I determined to tolerate what seemed like an inconvenient disability. But God wasn't content to leave it alone.

One morning while my family slept, I woke up early to read my Bible. In Genesis 45, the story of Joseph stirred me deeply. His words to his brothers showed how God could transform pain into good. "Oh God, I wish I could write down my thoughts about this story," I said, under my breath. Apparently he received this as a legitimate prayer request. I began my labored scribbling and swiftly realized I could write. And not only write, but with perfect fluidity.

"I can't believe this!" I said out loud.

The freedom lasted about two hours. I saved the papers, thinking no one would believe me otherwise. Later that afternoon, the familiar, paralyzed feeling returned. Nevertheless, a sense of awe floated over me like electrified air for several days, and I remained curious about it for months.

Then one hot day, during lunch with my pastor, I told him about my hand and the two-hour miraculous healing. "What do you make of that, Jim?" I asked.

"I think God gave you a little miracle to raise your faith." His Alabamian drawl had a rhythm, and sometimes just his voice put me at ease.

"Why would he want to raise my faith?" I scooped up ice cubes from my glass to melt in my mouth. I may have seemed nonchalant, but I was interested in the worst way.

"God wants to raise your faith to the point where you might believe he'll fully restore your hand." His eyes met mine straight on, but as he continued, he gazed over my head, envisioning something far-off and future. "And I think he plans to do just that."

"Really?" I said in disbelief, remembering the doctor's prognosis.

"Yes, and I believe that when he does heal you, it's a signal that he wants you to write for him. Maybe even a book. There's something significant about this."

I wasn't so sure. I mean, maybe I liked to journal. But he hadn't seen my SAT scores. If he had, he would have known I was a math person. He would have understood instantly that English grammar and writing were not my thing. Still, I mulled his words over as I left the restaurant.

The following January, my husband and I planned to visit a church in Canada that was reporting miracles similar to those during the Great Awakening. The day before we left, I had a vivid dream.

In the dream, a man stands next to the bed where I'm sleeping. He holds a pen and a stenographer's notebook, the kind with the spiral wire along the top. The man seems strong yet gentle, and he radiates authority. I am lying on my back in bed. The man takes a step forward and places the notebook and pen on my abdomen in a deliberate way. It's as if he is returning them and giving them to me at the same time.

The dream felt noteworthy. I jotted a description of it in my journal and elaborated on two things. First, the person in the dream had a Christ-like character, but I couldn't actually see his face. I had heard that this often represents the Holy Spirit. Second, the abdomen, or specifically the womb, signified a place of conception and birth. Intriguing symbolism, but I didn't know what else to make of it, so I left it there.

We departed the next day to visit the church in Toronto and stood outside in the cold, January air, queued up for hours just to get a seat. At the time, the church was renting a small space in a strip mall. While we waited, people from many different countries gathered by the entrance. Once the doors opened, some found seats, but quite a few people had to stand in the back and at the sides.

The worship started. When we sang "Holy, Holy, Holy," I heard the same song in many languages, sung in unison. A shiver came over me. *One day,* I thought, *this is how it will be…many tribes and tongues, together.*

A number of individuals told how God had healed various physical illnesses. The pastor invited people to come forward for prayer. A tug of war between faith and fear wrestled inside of me. Would I hold back and resist or go forward and trust? A decision had to be made.

I popped out of my chair and whisked my way down to the front. A small, fortyish woman approached me. She wore a bright orange badge that said, "Ministry Team" and placed her warm hand on my forearm. Her welcoming gesture melted away any pretense. After a few words of prayer, she stopped speaking as though interrupted.

"God sees you as an emotional doctor," she said. "You're someone he can use to help others who are wounded. Do you have a ministry?"

"I'm sort of a lay counselor." I'd been in that type of work for years. She prayed for God to increase my discernment. I also told her about my handwriting disability, and she prayed for my hand. There were no flashes of lightning, no collapsing on the floor. But over the next six months, my handwriting returned. Completely. God overruled the medical assumptions because he wanted to.

Nothing is too difficult for him.

Still, I had forgotten the words my pastor spoke months ago as I played with my ice water at the lunch table. I didn't have the faith or the vision to be a writer. Nine years passed, in fact, before I would take that first step to write for publication. But God didn't forget.

As I drove on Highway 302 through North Conway, New Hampshire, I thought of the night God had saved my life by sending a crazy rabbit.[8] He reminded me I was still on earth for a reason.

I was driving to a writers conference because I had entered a two-hundred-word piece in a writing contest. I had worked hard on the essay and sent it off before the deadline. Later, in the fine print of the brochure, I noticed that only those who attended the conference were eligible to win.

I could have ignored it. Felt cheated. Argued. But God was nudging me out of my small world. *Will you go? Will you step out of your protected territory into the unknown and surrender your self-doubt?* God asked the same questions I asked myself. I bought the plane ticket and reserved a rental car.

As I entered the hotel lobby, a staff member handed me a registration packet at the Welcome table. I opened it, and there before my eyes was a stenographer's notebook and a pen. They looked identical to the ones in my dream during an afternoon nap almost a decade ago.

My essay went on to win second place, and the following fall, my first feature article was published. A new journey had begun.

Where is God telling you to throw your net?

What is the God-given passion of your heart?

How will you use this wisp of time on earth?

These are vital, life-altering questions. And whatever leading you get, it will take untold courage to trust and act on it. But I can promise you that once you hear and respond, you'll never feel more alive. That's what my husband says about his work in Africa after leaving the business world.

Not long after the conference, these same questions came up in our Wednesday night home group. The responses were varied: Pepe felt called to work with the disabled. Peter saw himself as a steward of large amounts of money and resources that weren't his own like Joseph in Genesis. Erli expressed a passion for teens ensnared in the occult. Greg and Rina had overcome adultery and deep sexual sin issues. They knew God wanted them in marriage ministry. Jean is still waiting for her answer.

My turn came. There was no longer any hesitation. "God wants me to write."

And destiny can take you. Just like that.

FOURTEEN

Anchored
God as the Third Party in Marriage

There is, hidden or flaunted, a sword between the sexes till an entire marriage reconciles them.
—C. S. Lewis

Our guests stood up as the foyer doors swung open. Trembling with expectancy, I took my father's arm. He was steady. Organ music filled the sanctuary with rapturous sounds, and all heads turned toward me. We flowed seamlessly forward as though caught in the gentle current of a stream. As I passed each row, happy faces came in and out of my focus. The fragrance of my bouquet, the swish of satin, the beauty of the day all came together in one entrancing moment. We rounded the corner at the end of the aisle, and there stood my soon-to-be husband.

Duncan and I had practiced our vows the night before. He teased me, saying he couldn't memorize such a long marital pledge. He'd begin with "I, Susan, take you Duncan…" or halfway through he'd go blank and sum up the rest with "all the days of our lives." I knew he was playfully toying with me.

On our wedding day as we pronounced our vows before family and friends, he paused midway in his pledge. Mortified, I stopped breathing. With a glimmer in his eye, he whispered "all the days of our lives" and completed the remainder of his promise flawlessly. His added phrase was actually romantic in retrospect. Then a sparkling ring decorated my hand. A kiss on the lips, and we were man and wife. As we turned for the recessional, I now took my husband's arm.

Thinking back on that day, I marvel at how little we knew about the vows we made. How could we commit to such sweeping promises? Though weddings happen every day, each couple enters an unexplored, unknown experience, as unique as they are individually. No matter who you marry, you wake up next to someone different, someone who will change profoundly in the years to come.

Seven years later, our family gathered for my brother's rehearsal dinner. The next day, he would say those same all-encompassing vows to his bride. I sat between my grandmothers and held their soft, frail hands as we bowed our heads for prayer. Instead of closing my eyes, I looked at their hands and thought of their lifetimes of giving, soothing, mending, washing, and serving. Though wrinkled and delicate, they seemed worthy of the wedding rings they wore. Yet if my grandmothers had known on their wedding days what they would know a half century later, would they have taken the journey? I believed that if I asked them, their answers would be a resounding yes. For me, however, it posed a sobering question. Though I didn't know my life would come crashing down a month later, I felt a foreboding premonition that something was very wrong.

Marriage in its greatest moments is something otherworldly. Electrified feelings of romance color ordinary scenes of life like a Monet painting. Walking in the rain, sharing a meal, and other mundane experiences are transformed into times to remember, things to write about in a journal. Joined at the hip, newlyweds have few shadows in the sweet sunlight of new love.

With time, marriage evolves into an intimacy far richer than what you imagine you have in the beginning. Conversations deepen. Understanding and connection happen with just a glance. An encouraging word holds enormous power. Companionship soothes the weariness of a long day, when the need for quietness and retreat is shared. What can be said when your partner sees your imperfections, touches the ugly toes of your humanness, and loves you anyway? Sex is good because God blesses it. And there is something I can't find words for when together a husband and wife become one flesh in the form of a child.

So it was and is for us as a couple.

But marriage is also a crucible in the hardest and best sense of the word. Inherent in the blueprint of a lifelong commitment are both a severe test and a sovereign mercy. You either overcome your worst self, or you become it. In short, marriage is the context in which our imperfections become apparent. Marriage files off the self-centered edges and exposes the poser in all of us by revealing structural flaws that need repair. Pastor Francis Frangipane once said the Lord searches out a tailor-made spouse, perfectly designed to be your match—so God can kill you.[1] This is what Scripture calls *dying to self*.[2]

Most marriages go through cycles of death and resurrection, because as individuals we change. Soon we are not the same people we were at the altar, the people who said "I do" with utmost sincerity. Idiosyncrasies that once were mildly humorous become acutely annoying. Romance succumbs to familiarity. Stress at work, crying babies, financial worries, phones ringing, church needs, traffic jams, backed-up laundry, dinner messes, headaches…by the end of the day, your pillow may be more inviting than your spouse.

Unforeseeable hurts come. Angry words are said. Periods of silent alienation follow. And all this can lead to far worse for some. Maybe you're not the type to kick the cat, hang up on a solicitor, or yell at your spouse, but in the strenuous years of earning a living and raising a family, you can easily lose your way. Something dies inside. You can't put your finger on it, but there's a nagging sense of loss.

Yet staying committed in marriage makes the losses nothing more than shedding an old skin. Something passes away for something new to take its place. At times I marvel at the metamorphosis God works in people's lives. I see in Duncan a new man full of discernment, kindness, and generosity—ready for the adventure. I see a different man from the one who promised "all the days of our lives."

But so many couples seem unprepared for the dying part. They don't see anything beyond the disappointments they currently feel. They wonder if they've married the wrong person. Some simply want to *feel* in love again and seek it outside of marriage. Unfortunately, adultery is like drinking salt water, and it never satisfies the thirst. Unfaithfulness only creates more problems for the future.

Other couples choose to stay committed but grow increasingly disenchanted. They show up for dinner and share the same mailbox, but they are estranged. To survive, they back away from the intensity marriage creates and build emotional walls around their hearts. Wrapped in their pain, they begin to make secret decisions that oppose the union. Inner vows are powerful and binding. A hurting wife may declare to herself, *I'll never let him in again.* A shredded husband says in his heart, *See if I ever trust her again.* They may keep up a facade, but eventually, love starves to death.

When leveled by the pain of betrayal, I built a fortress around my heart. Death rattled over my broken marriage. I didn't realize God could bring about resurrection. A few years later, God gave me hope through the most vivid dream of my life. The scenes, in living color, enveloped me like a giant IMAX movie. I remember it clearly.

I'm swimming in a tropical paradise. Gorgeous sky-blue waters roll gently up a golden sandy beach. The temperature of sea and air feels perfect, and the warm sun caresses my skin. Delighted by the soft waves, I swirl in the surf with the energy of a seal. I'm in a state of unmatched tranquillity.

Eventually the waves carry me in to shore. Walking along the beach, I find a stone staircase that curves up a steep hillside and leads to an old stone cottage. As I near the top, I see an expansive view of the serene water below. I breathe deeply, invigorated by the exercise. Fresh air fills my lungs. I feel so healthy and notice my skin is pink and glowing from the sun. As soon as I enter the cottage, however, I experience all the sensations of ongoing battle.

The room is dark and clammy. I begin to feel slightly nauseated, as if I have eaten something deep fried. Pieces of potato chips are scattered around the floor. Duncan lies in a double bed, entangled in a black blanket as though he has tossed and turned all night. His hair is messy and he's unshaven. Dark circles under his eyes tell of his exhaustion.

Wanting to comfort him, I walk over to the bed and hand him a beautiful baby girl. She looks just like I did as a baby with light brown curls and pink cheeks. As I place her in Duncan's arms, his eyes grow wide and his entire expression brightens. He acts as if I've given him the most spectacular gift he's ever received.

Then the scene changes. I'm in a hotel room somewhere in Europe, unpacking my luggage with our two daughters. I slide into a white wedding dress. It's short and frilly unlike the traditional satin gown I actually wore. I'm about to remarry Duncan. Excitement fills the air as we prepare ourselves for the event. The girls run around the room as busy as squirrels. After a lady zips up my dress, I turn to view myself in the mirror and catch my breath. In my reflection, I look ten years younger.

The dream ended there, but I remained in bed, pondering the powerful images for almost an hour. I closed my eyes, hoping to reenter the dream. The scenes were stunningly real, as if I had truly been in that water, walked up those steps and encountered my husband in that gloomy bungalow. It was more than a bunch of random thoughts on the sleep-screen of my mind. God was giving me encouragement and instruction. As I wrote in my journal, the message became clear.

The ocean represented the endless presence and love of God. I felt so refreshed swimming in that lovely water. In real life, when marriage became a struggle, I sought solace in God. As it turned out, that's what he wanted anyway—he wanted me to spend time with him, absorbed in his vast comfort and affection.

Too often I relied on my spouse for a sense of security and happiness. I wanted Duncan to validate my worth and feed my contentment. How many times had I thought, "I'll be happy when…" How much time and energy was wasted, putting so much hope on another person to be there for me? But if my identity was anchored in God's love, if he was my source of well-being, I could be a different person. I'd be more stable and secure in relationships. I'd probably be a better wife.

When a person has a love deficit, oversensitivity abounds. After soaking in God's love, I didn't take things so hard. I could enter Duncan's world and understand that his battle was not my battle, experiencing his struggle but not internalizing it.

More important, God showed me that the best thing I could do for my husband was offer vulnerability and openness. Vulnerability is giving the gift of me. The baby girl was an image of this present. In my pain I desperately wanted to insulate my broken heart, but God asked me to do just the opposite: to give Duncan my true self and not shut down emotionally.

Choosing to stay real and available in marriage made me vulnerable. I risked rejection. Sometimes I had to make hard choices. I had to listen when I was furious, apologize when I was wrong, and forgive when I was hurt. It was much easier to stay angry, kill my heart, and let alienation reign. But God showed me, if I could stay open and receptive toward Duncan, our relationship would rise to a new level. We would "remarry" and enter a new season.

The message is true for my husband as well, because every struggle has two sides. I fight personal battles that are not his. He, in turn, must find God as his source. He also must choose to stay real in the relationship.

I thought about that dream many times in the years following, because the truths were so pivotal. Not long after, God reminded me of it again through a movie called *Contact*.[3]

Based on the novel by Carl Sagan, the movie is about a girl named Ellie Arroway, who loses both her parents to premature death. As a child, she yearns for communication with her deceased parents, wondering if there isn't some way to contact them.

As an adult, she joins a scientific team to search for extraterrestrial intelligence, seeking a higher power, something or someone to answer her deeper spiritual questions. Her boyfriend, Palmer, suggests that she's looking for God; she's not so sure.

One night, listening to satellite receivers, she hears a message from space. After translating it, the team discovers the message contains instructions for building a space machine that can carry a passenger far into space. The government decides to fund the project, and through various circumstances and disasters, Ellie is the only one eligible to go.

After eighteen hours of travel through wormholes and galaxies, she wakes up in a supernatural encounter. She stands on the sandy beach of a beautiful waterfront. Mystified, she waits for something to happen. Someone walks along the shore and gradually comes into focus. By all appearances, it is her father. He looks exactly like she remembered him. Undone by their reunion, her chin trembles and tears flow as they share a long embrace.

Soon she realizes it's not really her father. This alien of higher intelligence only looks like her father to make the situation more comfortable for her. She's bursting with questions, but his answers are elusive. Finally, he sums up their brief discussion, saying the only thing of importance in the universe is relationship.

As I heard these words, I let out a gasp. Jesus revealed the same conclusion to me in the teetertotter vision, when just like Ellie I felt deep grief in a broken world.

Picture it: a young woman in a paradiselike scene embraced by a higher power in father skin. She feels loved. She senses a connection to something bigger than her pain and suffering on earth. She finds hope. Isn't this exactly what God did when he came to us as Jesus? The God of the universe entered our realm in a living body so we could grasp his father love, so he could tell us relationship is all that matters. And on the beach of my dream, I felt all those same things as I swam in the ocean of his love. God touched me in a movie theater of all places.

God continued to talk to me through other images of that same dream. One morning while waiting in a doctor's office, I randomly picked up a news magazine and flipped pages. To my surprise, I turned the page and found a Caribbean water scene. Beautiful turquoise water filled the page with color. Two feet wearing flippers were in the foreground, as if the photographer had snapped a picture of his own feet. God was reminding me to swim in the sea of his great affection. Though I don't have any subscriptions to travel magazines, I continued to find pictures like this again and again in specific and timely ways.

When I bought a laptop, my son unknowingly picked a tropical ocean scene as the screensaver for my desktop. In other situations, my friends would ask with perfect timing, "Have you been swimming lately?" One could say these things are circumstance, random, or arbitrary. There's no reason behind it. It just is. But if you take the time to recognize the threads of God's voice, then words, images, dreams, and scriptures all blend into the mosaic of what he's already said. You begin to recognize God's inferences in the same way you can interpret a slightest glance from the person you know the best.

All this time God was teaching me crucial relationship principles. I couldn't give all that my marriage required without God as my source. Several years after the swimming dream, God used a new image to confirm that he stands with us in the ups and downs of marriage. Again, he spoke through a dream.

I'm standing at the back of a large conference hall looking for Duncan. I wait for a very long time. *Where is he?* Finally, the program is about to begin, and someone taps the microphone. The auditorium is packed, and people scurry to find a seat.

No sign of Duncan.

Finally, I see him coming through a side door. But something is different. He is six inches taller. He enters the great room with his eyes fixed on me, walking straight toward me. His face breaks into a smile. The mass of swarming people parts like the Red Sea to let him through. He reaches me and we embrace, holding each other as if we've been separated for ages. I look at him with admiration and new respect. He towers over me but his eyes are kind and gentle.

Suddenly my focus shifts. Duncan is transparent in a mystical kind of way, and I see Jesus standing right behind him. Jesus looks straight through Duncan's eyes at me. His expression is similarly compassionate. He understands what we've been through. His presence tells me, "I'm right here with you—both of you."

We are not alone. God is the third party in marriage. Our embrace, this scene of the three of us together, was indelibly imprinted on my heart. It remains as a picture of marriage as God created it to be—a wife respecting her husband, a husband loving his wife, and God standing with them, not even a hair's breath away.

FIFTEEN

Repairing Desolations
God Is All About Forgiveness

*Forgiveness is the
fragrance that the violet
sheds on the heel that has
crushed it.*

—MARK TWAIN

I n real life, the Cinderella story
doesn't end at the altar. The wedding is only the beginning of a radical transformation, wherein we have the potential to become more
than we would have been alone. Marriage is a prime venue for this
transformation, but the same applies to any relationship. This was, and
is, God's terrible good idea.

Unfortunately, pretty much everyone enters the process with wounds.
Some more than others. Would you climb a mountain with a broken leg
or run a marathon with a heart condition? Yet unseen injuries from our
tender years affect relationships as we get older. In marriage, they're particularly debilitating.

For example, a boy grows up with a controlling mother. At times he
feels close to her and confides his innermost feelings. She, in turn, uses
the information to shame him, sometimes publicly. The boy closes his
heart. Feeling betrayed, he vows never to trust a woman again.

Later the boy becomes a man and falls in love with a pretty girl. They flirt, talk, and kiss, experiencing an illusion of intimacy. Eventually they walk down the aisle and promise for better or worse. But one day, the wife jokingly criticizes her husband at an office party. Emotions and memories are triggered. The man projects his mother's betrayal onto his wife and guards his heart. His wife is bewildered. *Why won't he talk?* Instead, he retreats to his cave. He becomes emotionally distant much of the time. His instincts to shut down, back up, and hide are out of proportion to his wife's careless joke, all because a childhood wound remains unhealed.

In kindness, God brings our original wounds to the light of day. As children, we learned to survive the pain, but God doesn't want us to simply survive anymore. He wants healing. Marriage provides the catalyst for this process. While the truths in this chapter apply to all relationships, I learned about repair work initially with Duncan.

As you know, my marriage stumbled along for many years. At times, we remained committed for the kids' sake, hoping God would rekindle our feelings of love. Brokenhearted for many years, I was just surviving.

Gradually God taught me about original wounds. One doesn't have to be a trained psychologist to see how many problems transfer down generational lines. Abuse, alcoholism, adultery, perfectionism, bitterness, abandonment, incest, and other issues are patterns in families. God talked about this problem in the Old Testament. A father's sins will afflict his children and grandchildren. Sadly, this applies to families that hate God.[1] But there is hope for those who love God and follow his ways. The power of generational baggage and sin can be broken.

One morning while reading Isaiah, I came across an interesting phrase. The surrounding chapter paints a beautiful picture of restoration, but eight specific words seemed highlighted on the page: "they will repair…the desolations of many generations."[2] The text refers to rebuilding cities, but I knew there could also be a human subtext to the thought. Reconstructing external structures matters little if hearts are in disrepair.

God is always at work on more than one level when it comes to restoration. Could generational problems and sins be another meaning for the "desolation of generations"?

Like sticks of dynamite, wounds from our families were embedded in Duncan and me as we stood at the altar saying our vows. In our dating years, those wounds seemed benign because we were busy putting on our best selves. After the wedding, our hidden pains, idiosyncrasies, and dysfunctional patterns materialized.

At that point, we had two options: stalemate or humility. "Stale Mate," as Duncan calls it, is the result of blaming the other person and waiting for him or her to change. Humility is a willingness to look at your part in a problem and deal with things that shaped your life before you said "I do." And let it be known that God gives grace to the humble, but resists the proud.

Duncan and I were well down Stale-Mate Lane when God showed me another verse in Isaiah. As I read the passage, God poured a healing balm over my heartache:

> It will no longer be said to you, "Forsaken," nor to your land will
> it any longer be said, "Desolate"; but you will be called, "My
> delight is in her," and your land, "Married"; for the LORD
> delights in you, and to Him your land will be married.[3]

Through two verses in Isaiah, God gave me a word of instruction and a word of promise: *first repair the desolation of generations...and then your land will be called "Married."* It seemed that God was making an "if you will, then I will" kind of statement. Many prophecies are made like this in the Bible.[4] God was bringing us to the threshold of action.

Marital pain crippled us in broader ways, undermining our parenting, our work, and even our health. It was time to do something. We confided in Jack, a pastor and friend from Whitefish, Montana. He had driven down to shoot skeet with my husband for a few days. Over dinner, he recommended that we see his friend John, a professional counselor in Fort Worth.

Within a month, we set aside a whole week and left for Texas. We arrived in the evening and drove silently to a hotel. Once in our room, I crawled under the covers and kept to myself, afraid and emotionally fragile.

That night God gave me a dream I now call the Texas Highway Dream. I will never forget it: Duncan and I are traveling in two different cars on the interstate surrounding Dallas/Fort Worth. Our cars are side by side, when suddenly we come to a spaghetti tangle of exit ramps and overpasses. By all accounts, this intersection is a construction feat.

Marveling at the enormous serpentine configuration before us, we fail to realize what's about to happen. Because we're in different lanes, we suddenly separate. I stay on the main road, but Duncan unintentionally exits off to the right.

I'm stunned by the mishap. Beyond any rationality, I believe I've lost my husband forever. Grief descends like a sudden cloudburst, and I weep profusely. My chest heaves and swells with great sighs. I can barely see the road. But after a while, my raw emotions settle, and I drive along, contemplating my sad dilemma.

Wiping my eyes, I see a massive, ten-story structure, far away on the skyline. As I get closer, it appears to be a giant monument carved in granite. All at once, I realize the monument is the word "ISAIAH" in huge block letters. I know Duncan will see it too. No matter how many miles separate us, we will eventually meet here.

As I awoke in our hotel room, tears trickled down the side of my face. Comfort hovered over the bed. There was something so kind about the dream. Two important verses in Isaiah were written in stone on the horizon of my struggle. I knew that God was speaking to me.

The next morning, while traveling on the interstate to the counselor's office, we suddenly came to a massive web of highway overpasses *exactly* like the one I had seen in my dream. My mouth hung open. I stuttered to find words, pointing toward the junction. I'd never seen anything like it in real life. I told Duncan about the dream, and he was astonished too.

When we arrived at the counselor's office, I asked about the interchange. "Yes, isn't that something?" John said. He knew what I was talking about before I finished the question. Apparently, that four-level stack of roads called the Mixmaster was the first of its kind in Texas back in the 1950s. Though it's been rebuilt since then, it remains an engineering spectacle.[5]

Yes, the Mixmaster was amazing. But even more astounding was the mystery of seeing it in a dream before I saw it on the Fort Worth highway. I felt stirred by the Holy Spirit. I knew that soon he would interpret the message of the dream.

After a long, intense week of counseling, John concluded that we didn't have serious marital troubles. He said our problems were individual, and we needed to work on them separately. Our issues predated our marriage and related to our families of origin. To blame and accuse each other was counterproductive. He gave us some guidelines for communication, but he explained that as we healed individually, our marriage would also heal.

I was speechless, shaking my head. The dream portrayed a symbolic summary of his diagnosis. Driving tandem on a straight road, our early marriage sent us in the same direction, but we were still not united. The journey became increasingly complicated with stress at work, three young children, and bills to pay. We had entered the Mixmaster stage of life and abruptly found ourselves on separate paths. I was devastated. But as we worked individually through our own problems, our marriage would heal and our roads would ultimately merge. Solid and firm as a mountain of stone, the two verses in Isaiah were God's instruction and his promise: *First repair the desolation of generations, then your land will be called, "Married."*

Seeing the Mixmaster in a dream before I saw it on the highway was an important part of the message. Something could be real even before

I saw it with my own eyes. In the same way, healing was possible for us, though we couldn't envision it yet. In this way, God imparted hope to me, and hope was what I needed to continue by faith.

I don't know how anyone does marriage without God. The apostle Paul made it sound easy when husbands love their wives and wives respect their husbands. But living it out is another thing.

We returned home and agreed to work on our own issues. Meanwhile, we practiced a constructive form of communication John called safe talk.[6] For the time being, peace replaced strife.

Repairing the desolation of generations came down to the hard work of forgiveness. To start, we examined the ways we were affected by our families, but not as an exercise in parent bashing. Some hurtful things happened inadvertently and were more a matter of perception than actuality. Still, some things were real and not imagined. We felt like God asked us to look to the past with more compassion and less judgment, because our grandparents, parents, siblings, and others were wounded people too.

Childhood wounds basically fell into two categories—things that were done to us and things that we needed but didn't get. One could spend months or years pouring out past sorrows to a counselor, wallowing in self-pity, and still not get anywhere. Though others helped us, we found that the Holy Spirit was the best counselor. He brought to remembrance the pertinent things that created our original wounds.

When someone is hurt, a series of responses come into play. At a shallow level, one feels anger and resentment (for example: Dad yelled at me. Now I'm mad). If the hurt goes deeper, sometimes judgments are made (Dad is a mean jerk). If the hurt happens often or for a long duration, someone may make an inner vow (I'll never love Dad again). And most distressing, a lie can sprout from the deepest wounds, tainting one's perception of life (Men cannot be trusted).[7]

Restoration began when we asked God to reverse the fallout of our pain-driven responses. First, we asked the Holy Spirit to show us our resentments. Next, we became willing to forgive those who hurt us and apologize for any judgments we made against them. Then we asked God to break the power of any inner vows that were made, spoken or unspoken. Understanding the judgments and vows proved to be the most telling part of the process. In the end, God exposed the lies we believed and replaced them with his truth.

My husband and I worked individually, not together. In addition, our forgiveness work didn't involve the people who caused us pain. The process took a few years, as most of our original wounds were revealed in layers. God knew how much we could bear. Grieving each loss was important in order to let go of the past. We asked friends and counselors to pray with us when it came to judgments and vows. They also helped us see the wound-based lies we believed. It was hard emotional work, but it brought about much healing.

The power of forgiveness cannot be overstated. It breaks patterns. Perhaps you've heard the saying—the way a man treats his mother is an indication of how he will respond to his wife. If a man hates his mother and treats her badly, it is likely he will repeat the behavior on his wife. But if he examines the original hurt, forgives his mother, retracts the judgments he made against her, and breaks any misogynistic vows, he is set free to love his wife.

In the same way, a woman who rebels against her father will not treat her husband with respect if original issues remain unexamined. Given the human condition, relationships need forgiveness like plants need water and sunlight. But it's crucial to begin with the past, focusing on the first relationships of life.

Duncan and I made huge strides because our forgiveness work was intentional. As a result, we progressed on the journey of marriage. God continued to be the anchor of our well-being. He sustained us with his encouragement through scriptures, dreams, symbolic coincidences, impressions, and the like. Without hope for a healed marriage, we would have wandered aimlessly and lost our resolve.

God recently affirmed our long hard road to restoration. As you know, over twenty years ago I literally lost my diamond in our backyard garden and miraculously found it again. The same thing happened later in a dream. I not only found my diamond, but other gems as well. In the dream, I took them to Duncan, because I knew he would make a new wedding ring. Recently, my husband said he wanted to do just that. I balked at the idea, feeling sentimental about my wedding ring. But then I remembered the dream.

When we were first engaged, we couldn't afford a solitaire diamond like the ones you see on TV commercials. My original engagement ring was a thin gold band with one inlaid diamond. The stone was tiny, like a crystal of sea salt. My husband's idea was to add a little diamond to the band for each year we were married.

Later, my mother-in-law gave us a solitaire diamond for a classic engagement ring, so I wore both. Duncan put a plain gold wedding band on my finger during the ceremony. I wore the solitaire diamond ring next, and the original engagement ring last, making it the *guard ring*— an interesting term, if you think symbolically like me. We added a tiny stone to the guard ring each year as planned.

On our fourth anniversary, however, Duncan asked the jeweler to insert a tiny sapphire instead, thus starting a pattern of three diamonds, one sapphire, followed by three diamonds and so on. Every few years, we added the little gems to bring my guard ring up to date. Bear with me now, because here's where it gets interesting.

When Duncan said he wanted to make me a new ring, it was our twenty-eighth anniversary. We hadn't been to the jeweler in a while, so Duncan wanted to add a few more stones to the guard ring, making twenty-eight in all.

The jeweler turned my guard ring around and around in her fingers, looking closely with magnifying glasses. With some kind of tool, she measured and calculated. She shook her head and measured again. Finally

she announced, "This never happens." Bewildered, we stood there thinking, *What?*

"The ring will hold *precisely* twenty-eight stones." She explained that
with the variables of stone and ring sizes, a ring like this usually ends up
with an odd space. That's the problem with adding one or two stones at
a time. You can't make it come out right. "But that's not what's amazing,"
she said, rotating the ring in her hand once again to be sure. "What's
amazing is that twenty-eight stones complete the pattern. That makes it
an eternity ring." In her opinion, *that never happened.* Apparently an eternity ring has to be designed from the start or the pattern won't finish. Yet
building stone after stone, the pattern on my ring came out perfect.

As Duncan often asks, "Was it odd or was it God?" In my mind,
God was saying something through the completion of my ring. When
you think of a guard ring, it's the last one you put on your finger to protect the loss of your wedding rings. Each stone represented a hard-won
year of marriage. The finished pattern formed a visual symbol of something eternal, something lasting. I could almost hear the Lord saying,
Now your land will be called "Married," echoing the promise he gave to
me in a Texas hotel room years ago.

But even beyond the hope of symbols and signs, I now feel and see
the changes. For the first time in our married life, we are able to work
together in the same office. That alone is a miracle. When my husband
started a nonprofit organization in 2002 to build orphan homes in
Uganda, he badly needed an administrator. Other women volunteered.
They came and went for various reasons, but God reserved the role for
me. We're learning that our vastly different approaches (read: like oil and
water) are actually complementary. He's a big-picture guy, and I think
out the details, yet we've come to value the differences that used to
divide us.

I believe a rich blessing is reserved for husbands and wives who overcome in marriage. There's no easy button, no "Stepford spouse" way to

eliminate the otherness of the other. But marriage is God's idea, and so we are not alone in our efforts.

While marriage is often the central relationship in adulthood, these same ideas apply to all relationships. God challenges us to honor our parents, respect those in authority, and not exasperate our children. We have neighbors to live by and associates to work with. Some of us have difficult relatives. And don't forget to welcome the stranger and care for widows and orphans. Human relationships are predictably messy. They make apologies and forgiveness necessary. They require humility. But God will give us guidance along the way. When I consider all the ways God encouraged me in marriage, I'm convinced that he will help me in any relationship.

God is all about forgiveness, reconciliation, and restoration. Even in the agony of Jesus's death he said, "Father, forgive them; for they do not know what they are doing." [8] While God loves people, he hates bitterness, judgment, and the fallout of broken relationships. Scripture says we can't be close to God and at odds with people. [9] It just doesn't work that way. To truly know God, we must love what he loves and hate what he hates. To find intimacy with him, we must agree with the foundation of his kingdom—forgiving others because God has forgiven us.

SIXTEEN

No Stones or Snakes
Parenting with God

How many hopes and fears, how many ardent wishes
and anxious apprehensions are twisted together in the threads
that connect the parent with the child!
—SAMUEL GRISWOLD GOODRICH

I n April 1999 the Family Research Council printed a poignant essay by Dale Hanson Bourke called, "The Price of Motherhood: A Two-Hankie Perspective." The author describes having lunch with a friend, who mentions that she and her husband are thinking about having a baby. Her friend's biological clock is counting down, compelling her to mull over the idea of motherhood.

"It will change your life," I say carefully, keeping my tone neutral.

"I know," she says. "No more sleeping in on Saturdays, no more spontaneous vacations…"

But that is not what I mean at all. I look at my friend, trying to decide what to tell her.

I want her to know what she will never learn in childbirth classes. I want to tell her that the physical wounds of childbirth heal, but that becoming a mother will leave her with an emotional wound so raw that she will be forever vulnerable.

I consider warning her she will never read a newspaper again without asking, "What if that had been my child?"…That when she sees pictures of starving children, she will look at the mothers and wonder if anything could be worse than watching your child die.

I look at her carefully manicured nails and stylish suit and think she should know that no matter how sophisticated she is, becoming a mother will immediately reduce her to the primitive level of a she-bear protecting her cub.… I want her to know that however decisive she may be at the office, she will second-guess herself constantly as a mother. …

My friend's relationship with her husband will change, I know, but not in the ways she thinks. I wish she could understand how much more you can love a man who is always careful to powder the baby or who never hesitates to play "bad guys" with his son.…

I hope she will understand why I can think rationally about most issues, but become temporarily insane when I discuss the threat of nuclear war to my children's future.

I want to describe to my friend the exhilaration of seeing your son learn to hit a baseball. I want to capture for her the belly laugh of a baby who is touching the soft fur of a dog for the first time. I want her to taste the joy that is so real that it hurts.

My friend's quizzical look makes me realize that tears have formed in my eyes. "You'll never regret it," I say finally.…I offer a prayer for her and me and all the mere mortal women who stumble their way into this holiest of callings.[1]

That's only part of it, but each time I read this piece, I dissolve into tears. I can feel the raw emotional wound she describes so accurately. Bourke conveys what many mothers feel all around the world.

Being a parent has changed my life forever. I felt enchanted by my infant daughter's faint smiles and delighted with her first laugh. How I savored the sweet smell of her fuzzy head. With each baby came new discoveries. I loved the worldview of their four-year-old minds as they formulated the most interesting questions: "Is snow a milk product?" and "How do shoes untie themselves?" Or, "If there are AA meetings, are there BB and CC meetings too?" And, "Why doesn't it tickle when you tickle yourself?"

I remember climbing into the hammock one cool fall evening with Sarah and Nate, our younger two. We were all peas and carrots, snuggled together inside two sleeping bags zipped together reading a bedtime story. Sarah grew wiggly, because she had heard the Berenstain Bear tales hundreds of times. She crawled deep into our makeshift cocoon to stay warm and began tickling my feet. I moved my legs over to get out of her reach, but she pursued them relentlessly. I swung my feet to the edge of the bag, but she was determined. Finally, her weight tipped the balance, and she plunged off the hammock, flipping us over with her.

The sound of three bodies in a sleeping bag hitting the deck made a loud but muffled thud. It took us a few seconds to realize what had happened. Soon the hilarity of the moment took over. We laughed uncontrollably. You know the kind of uproarious guffaw you get in a library where you're supposed to be quiet? But there was no suppressing it that night. We let loose with abandon for a full ten minutes. Three human lumps in a double-wide green pod, racked with laughter, and too weak to stand up.

Without a doubt, children are a glorious, miraculous gift. Yet parenting isn't easy. We live in a time when you have to be concerned about your five-year-old son going into the bathroom at a department store by himself. In the grade school years, I rarely let my daughters walk home from the bus stop, even though we lived in a small town.

Now as a parent of teens, a whole new level of worry occupies my waking thoughts: mainstream drug use, X-rated rap lyrics, low-cut jeans, the intrigue of the "bad boy," and movie-driven casual sex, to mention a few. How about the "your truth isn't my truth" skepticism toward religion or the culture of disrespect in high-school hallways?

Even kids who go to Christian schools are at risk. Some high-school boys explained this to me one Saturday morning over breakfast. They said their school was like a restrictive playpen. In their view, administrators and teachers enforced persnickety rules with a "can't do this, can't do that" mentality. A Christian pledge kids said at the beginning of each school day became a rote religious exercise, meaningless to most of them. A lot of students attended only because their parents chose it for them. Bored with Bible study, they rolled their eyes at many of the chapel speakers who presented monotonous, worn-out themes. Worst of all, if kids were overtaught to be good, it became cool to be bad. Their sobering insights impacted me, and I believed them.

Then one night, a teen game show came on the Christian TV channel. I was just about to turn in for bed, but something about the young contestants hooked me. The game involved two teams playing Bible trivia. One group consisted of three girls from the same family. They were homeschooled and bore a family resemblance. Wearing identical T-shirts and jeans, they even sported similar nondescript hairstyles. Each girl was introduced and briefly interviewed:

"So, what do you do in your spare time?" the host asked the middle sister.

"I like to watch *VeggieTales*."

"Oh c'mon now, your little sister just said that. What do *you* really like to do?"

"Well, um, I really like *VeggieTales*."

"And how about you, young lady. You must be the oldest. What are your interests after your homework is done?

"I like to watch *VeggieTales*."

"You're joking, right?"

"No, I really do. We all really like *VeggieTales*." Apparently, the only differentiation between them was age.

The other team consisted of one girl and two guys, all from different families. The girl looked slightly irreverent, her head tilted with attitude. Bangs slanted over her mascara eyes. She dressed in the push-up bra, slinky shirt, and tight pants style of today and said her friends were "everything." One of the boys was decked out Goth style, and the other was into punk music. Both guys had conspicuous biblical names. When the host introduced one as Noah, he looked at the ground with fiery red cheeks. Their demeanor burned with an edgy negativity.

The contest appeared to be a battle between the "bad" Christian kids and the "good" ones. And as expected, the "good" Christian kids consistently chirped the right answers and won the game.

Has it come down to this kind of polarization? Do we either clone our kids to be safer than sorry or risk their need for individuality in a disturbing culture? Do we hold them tightly in the beginning and release them gradually in the teen years? If so, how soon, how fast, and how much?

Parenting certainly isn't for the faint of heart. With each passing year, the complex job of motherhood became increasingly daunting.

As I did in other areas of my life, I tried raising my kids in my own human strength and wisdom. Being a good parent, I thought, was a rather long paragraph in the "good Christian" job description. It was something *I did,* with the hope that God would say, "Good job!" in the end. Initially, I didn't recognize how much I needed God.

Often I felt depleted just teaching my kids basic common courtesies: things like respecting private property and asking before you borrow something, not to mention countless little considerations like using coasters or replacing the toilet paper roll. Parenting was strenuous most days. Some evenings, I collapsed in a heap on the couch as soon as the dinner dishes were done.

Leading authorities have written wonderful, comprehensive books on parenting, and I've read some of the best. Yet raising children isn't formulaic. I easily did the right thing in the wrong situation and the wrong thing in the right situation. And speaking as one raised by loving, stable parents, how much harder is it for my fellow parents who grew up under screaming mothers and alcoholic fathers? Even so, my best intentions seemed inadequate for the task.

I soon found intimacy with God was paramount. Over the years, God gave Duncan and me countless words of instruction, warnings, and encouragement at important junctures. His words came to us through scriptures, other people, dreams, coincidences, and ordinary circumstances. God spoke as the still small voice Isaiah prophesied:

> He…will no longer hide Himself, but your eyes will behold your Teacher. Your ears will hear a word behind you, "This is the way, walk in it," whenever you turn to the right or to the left.[2]

Over time, we recognized God's voice and learned to parent with him. After all, he's the original Parent. Why not go to the source? As Jesus said,

> What man is there among you who, when his son asks for a loaf, will give him a stone? Or if he asks for a fish, he will not give him a snake, will he? If you then, being evil, know how to give good gifts to your children, how much more will your Father who is in heaven give what is good to those who ask Him![3]

God is not offering us stones or snakes. We're only twisting in the wind if we don't seek his wisdom, and even then, God is at work. When I came to the end of my best efforts as a parent, I asked for help. It went like this: "Help!" Simple enough, yet I had to give the word a little push with my tongue to get it out. But this is a 911 kind of prayer that God loves to answer.

Eighteenth-century mother Susanna Wesley understood 911 prayers. She gave birth to nineteen children. Consider the stunning fact that she was pregnant for more than fourteen years of her adult life (I did the math). That alone was reason enough to desperately need God's help. But that's not all. As a mother, she had cause for anguish far beyond the trials of many modern women. Half of her babies died in childbirth, her husband spent extended time in debtor's prison, their house burned to the ground, and one of her daughters became pregnant out of wedlock. Yet in the busy commotion of her home, she found a corner, and—get this—pulled her hoop skirt over her head. Definitely a clear signal to her children that she needed time alone with God. In those moments, she sought wisdom from above.

Doesn't it make you want a hoop skirt? Yet even without one I can find a corner, a quiet place with God, where he gives me hope, instruction, and encouragement. He is there for all weary and discouraged parents.

God is working off the clock, day and night. He also works weekends, by the way. He is the truth teller when we have to bite our tongues. He provides that supernatural covering we call angelic protection. He goes where we can't go with omniscient awareness, a gift I would like to have on Friday and Saturday nights. He is the unseen, sovereign parent. Hagar said he is the God who sees. David said he is the God who hears. Elihu said God is behind all things, "whether for correction, or for His world, or for lovingkindness, He causes it to happen." Consider the "wonders of one perfect in knowledge." God puts wisdom in our innermost being and gives understanding to our minds. He even invites our 911 prayers, saying, "Call to Me and I will answer you, and I will tell you great and mighty things, which you do not know." [4] All I needed was a corner.

Rewind to August 8, 1983, the beginning of my parenting adventure. Duncan and I held a tiny girl with rosebud lips. We wept for the sheer glory of God embodied in a fragile infant. Driving home from the hospital, terrible postpartum blues mushroomed like a dark cloud over me. I realized in retrospect this was largely hormonal. But then I wondered how

God could give me something as perfect as a baby and expect me to raise her in such a messed-up world. The smelly exhaust fumes of traffic, the noise of honking horns, and the litter on the street bothered me now as a mother. Sorrow streamed out of my eyes in unending tears.

My own kind mother sat next to me in the front seat, touching my arm, soothing me with words as we drove from the hospital to the house. Later when my husband came home, he listened to my heartfelt burden and studied me with gentle eyes. His face looked perplexed as he made an effort to understand the intensity of my emotions. He assured me with thoughtful words, and I felt a little better.

But when I climbed into bed that night, God spoke to me through his Word. Flipping through Isaiah, my eyes landed on "nursing child." I stopped and read the whole verse:

> Can a woman forget her nursing child and have no compassion
> on the son of her womb? Even these may forget, but I will not
> forget you. Behold, I have inscribed you on the palms of My
> hands.[5]

The blues began to fade away. Though my heartstrings were finely tuned to a little baby sleeping in the next room, God was near, speaking into my spirit with carefully chosen words. Postpartum depression can be far more debilitating for some. Yet trusting God with the future gave me hope. He wouldn't forget me. In my life, parenting would inescapably demand a new level of faith. But God would come through and take the journey with me.

SEVENTEEN

Steadfast Love
Still Parenting with God

In the wilderness...you saw how
the Lord your God carried you,
just as a man carries his son.
—MOSES, DEUTERONOMY 1:31

God is actively involved in our circumstances, though it's natural to wonder if life is just random. At times we feel tossed around by huge waves on a sea of chaos. But God is everywhere, and he knows everything. He said so through David in Psalm 139 and many other scriptures.

But he also said so to me. One morning when my kids were still young, I dreamt that Jesus knelt by my bedside and whispered a secret in my ear. In a calm voice he said, "Susan, I'm sovereign over the tiniest little things." The experience was so lucid that I immediately opened my eyes, expecting to see him there.

Why bother believing in God at all if he doesn't have unlimited power and all-seeing knowledge? A God who knows what he's doing is worth seeking out, and that's why a relationship with him is all important.

And building intimacy with him requires nothing so much as paying attention. How easily we delete his messages like junk mail. We're chronically distracted. The noise of earthly life commandeers our waking thoughts. The blaring TV, the demands of work, an obstinate child, unread e-mails—it's a wonder hoop skirts haven't come back into fashion. We need a quiet space to hear him whether we realize it or not.

Soon the weighty responsibility of parenting brought me to a not-so-quiet desperation for God. I eagerly watched for his signals, because life with kids presented innumerable challenges. To my relief, God responded in a variety of ways.

For example, when our older daughter Katie was about nine, Wish Trolls with crystal belly buttons hit the stores as the hot new toy. Crystal worship had gained cultural popularity, assigning spiritual power to mere stones. Katie wanted the cute-ugly figures because they had hair. The shiny stones were not important to her.

I had just read a parenting article by author Frank Peretti in which he addressed the spiritual messages associated with some toys. The article couldn't have been timelier. Peretti suggested that, rather than taking those Ninja Turtles (or Wish Trolls) away from children, parents should ask their kids if the toys really have power. If they do, where do they get it? He suggested using the toys as a springboard to talk about real supernatural forces—both good and bad. Peretti emphasized teaching discernment instead of reacting with legalism.[1] Preparing our children to interpret the mixed messages of a secular culture is far more vital than controlling the situation or using punishment instead. Through this one article, God prompted me to have many such teachable moments with my children.

The Wish Troll dilemma was one of hundreds of gray areas. Toys, clothing, music, and movies constantly tested our wisdom as parents. But we knew that Christian legalism can be more toxic in parenting than cultural pressures. Our counselor, John, said that the most destructive family type isn't the physically abusive kind, as implausible as that seems. Even more perilous, John maintained, are religious parents who set exceedingly high standards for behavior but fail to show their children any process of growth. In this scenario, the parents seem perfect and the kids feel like failures. Unable to attain the high bar of piety, children begin believing something is wrong with them. This dynamic in religious families is particularly vicious if the parents are unaffectionate and rigid.

Personally, I might have thrown Wish Trolls into the no-way category. Instead, I asked God: *Help me on this one, Father.* You see, Christian fear mongering tells us to avoid the big, bad world at all costs. Follow that line of thinking and before long, as C. S. Lewis said, "The list of things forbidden will increase, till to get through a single day without supposed sin becomes like an elaborate step-dance."[2] In the end, we bought our daughters the trolls, and *they* peeled off the "crystals" and threw them away.

Only God can help us find the balance, shaping our children to be in the world, not of it. There's a time to say yes and teach discernment but also a time to say no and draw a clear line. In parenting, only God can show you when is when. You have to stop, ask, and listen. Sometimes you know his answer is "Yes" because you feel a perfect peace. Other times, a "No" may feel like a body block. Occasionally his "No" is a flashing-red-light kind of warning. And every so often you sense a "Wait" message, like a kind hand on your shoulder. Usually God confirms his short answers (yes, no, wait) in other ways, especially when it involves important decisions.

When Sarah was a toddler, she struggled with a phenomenon called night terrors. Medical doctors have various theories about it, but they generally file it under "GORK" (God Only Really Knows). People in a night terror seem stuck in a nightmare, and you can't wake them up. The next day, they have no memory of the incident. One night Sarah screamed in terror, calling for me in the dark. I held her, saying, "I'm right here!" but she couldn't hear me.

Around the same time, Katie had a recurring dream about a manlike, dark being who walked up our driveway every night. He looked like a drifter, and she sensed something sinister about him. In her dream, he came to sit on the electrical power box by Sarah's bedroom. My husband understood from Katie's dream that Sarah's night terrors were a spiritual attack. Each time she cried out in the night, I ran to hold her, but Duncan instinctively got on his knees to pray. When he did, she calmed down immediately and slept peacefully the rest of the night. Soon we asked the elders of our church to pray through our home. After that, Katie's dream and Sarah's night terrors both ended. Through this experience and others, we were learning a lesson about spiritual warfare and the power of prayer.

God also warned us through many dreams that our daughters' teenage years would be rough. One dream seems particularly prophetic now in retrospect.

In the dream, the girls are standing next to me, one on each side. With my arms around their slender waists, we prepare to cross a ten-lane highway at rush hour. The traffic is thick, and people are driving chaotically. We can only manage one lane at a time, pausing on the white-dashed lines. Safe passage will require patience, courage, and sheer faith, because the situation feels as dangerous as a cattle stampede. We navigate about four lanes when, unexpectedly, Sarah rushes out on her own, attempting something like a fifty-yard dash to cross the remaining stretch. She makes it to the sixth lane and disappears into the herd of cars. I sense she's been hit, but a green van blocks my view.

The dream ended abruptly, and I woke up in a cold sweat.

I knew it was a big mistake to take scenes and images too literally. Neither did I want to overanalyze the details or get fanatical about an application. From studying biblical dreams, I knew they commonly had one central message embedded in a general theme.

Here the highway symbolized the fast-paced intensity of today's world. The ten lanes represented the ten precarious preteen and teenage years that lay ahead of our daughters. My role was to help them traverse this road of life, one year at a time. If the girls stayed with me (and Duncan), they'd cross unharmed. But if they ran ahead, they faced dangers. God stirred me to pray for them.

Soon after, he reminded me of the prodigal son story in Luke 15. Bringing children to adulthood involves letting them separate from you. Individuation is necessary to growth and maturity. I felt God was warning me about Sarah yet comforting me as a parent. I was moved by two things in the story: the steadfast love of the father but also the elder-brother syndrome.

Despite any claims to the contrary, kids raised in Christian families inevitably enter a season when they must decide for themselves what they believe. Some make this transition at a young age, others in the turbulent years of high school. Many kids don't approach the threshold of faith until long after they leave the nest. And sadly, some never do. Personally, I'm more concerned about the good son or daughter who postpones this decision until midlife, and then has a crisis of faith far more destabilizing than teenage defiance.

During this transition, there are two kinds of prodigals. The external prodigal questions his family's faith and lifestyle and is often morally compromised. This son or daughter is the classic rebellious kid. To some extent, all teenagers spend a fair amount of energy saying, "I'm not you—I'm me." It's normal. Problems come when they make a career out of it.

But the second type of prodigal is the elder brother. His struggle is internal and often hidden from others. He goes along with the religious program and acts like a Christian but may live a double life. He doesn't embrace his parents' faith as his own, and as an adult he may stop attending church and only celebrate Christmas and Easter for the sake of tradition. Growing up in a religious environment but missing the relationship with God creates a dangerous spiritual deficit.[3] Our daughters would struggle in both ways.

In the story, the father's response was unwavering love. He knew one would go away, and he let him go. He knew the other would stay and question his ways. He understood their different struggles, and yet remained steadfast in his great affection. He believed the best for his sons and waited by faith with ready, open arms.

Through this beautiful parable, God taught me not to corner my kids spiritually. On moral issues I taught them right from wrong, but with spiritual matters I made room for their questions. God used Albert Schweitzer's wise words in *Memoirs of Childhood and Youth* to stretch my understanding. Schweitzer admitted his teenage years were a time of unpleasant fermentation working itself off to leave the wine clear.[4] He continues, telling of his inward prodigal journey:

> [For religious instruction] I was sent to old Pastor Wennagel, for
> whom I had a great respect. But to him…I kept myself closely
> shut up. I was a diligent candidate, but the good man never sus-
> pected what was stirring in my heart. His instruction was in itself
> excellent, but it gave no answer to a great deal of what my inner
> self was concerned with. How many questions I would gladly
> have asked him. But that was not allowed us.… He wanted to
> make us understand that in submission to faith all reasoning
> must be silenced.[5]

I resonated with Schweitzer's sentiments. In my youth, I kept many spiritual queries to myself. It felt disrespectful to question my faith or God openly. As a parent, I wanted to change this taboo. I resisted saying, "This is what *we* believe." Instead I'd say, "This is what *I* believe. What do you think about it?" Teens and young adults don't just need a secure setting to sort out their beliefs. They also want parents, pastors, and teachers to acknowledge that faith is ultimately their choice.

Several years after the Ten-Lane-Crossing dream, Sarah dashed out and took a hit in real life. In high school, she began abusing alcohol. Though she tried to keep it a secret, God talked to me about it one night in another dream.

In my dream, I see Sarah auditioning on a stage. Sarah is a songbird, constantly acting and singing some rendition of a musical or a play. As I watch her sing, a muscular, bare-chested man uses a giant shepherd's hook to pull her offstage, like they did on the *Gong Show.* He looks like a menacing version of Mr. Clean. Apparently I think this is a good time to chat with God. Still in the dream I ask,

"What's the hook, Lord?"

"Alcoholism." He says it straight up.

"Who is the strong man over there, the one holding the hook?"

"His name is Deception, and they work together." God doesn't mince words, but continues with encouragement. "However, if she overcomes, I have *this* for her."

Immediately, a Jacob's ladder type of beanstalk rises up under my feet, carrying me far into the sky. The lift was breathtaking, and jolted me out of sleep. Whether I saw Jacob's ladder or Jack's beanstalk, it symbolized a direct connection between heaven and earth. It represented a place of God's favor and great spiritual activity. I knew God had designs on Sarah.

Most often, God gives a dream so we will pray. Great power is released when we pray into reality what God wants for our lives. In Quixotian language, is it not madness to only see what is and fail to pray for what should be? Maybe we dream impossible dreams, but if God is behind the warning and the promise, anything is feasible. Prayers are often the landing pad for God to intervene on the earth. So I prayed God would defeat the strong man called Deception and his hook called Alcoholism and found support for this in Jesus's teaching.[6] I prayed also that my daughter would come into the fullness of God's plans for her.

Yes, I ran around in frantic-parent mode sometimes. We had curfews and grounded her. We asked her to go to AA meetings and set up appointments with counselors. We even confronted her friends. Yet all that didn't make much difference. She had already made a prodigal decision that she would have to sort out. I learned that prayer was far more powerful than hysterical antics. What comforted me was the fact that God knew about Sarah's choices in advance and told me so. I knew he watched and waited with me.

I could tell you numerous stories about parenting with God, but the exciting part comes when your children make their own connections with him. For example, in *Home Alone,* Kevin loses his family and prays to a Christmas tree for help.[7] My son, Nate, only five, leaned over and whispered that Christmas trees don't have any power. Score: God: 1; Christmas trees: 0.

This spring, Sarah and her friend Danelle went swimming in the Boulder River. They had traveled several miles on a four-wheeler to get there. Wading into waist-high water, they suddenly realized they had made a mistake. The river was treacherously cold, and they could easily slip into hypothermia. Shivering and scared, they returned to the four-wheeler, but the key was missing. Danelle's cabin was at least an hour-and-a-half walk away. She started to cry. Sarah decided it was time to pray, and together they asked God for help. Danelle said, "I'll believe in God if you find the key."

Now, I don't know if that was testing God. Then again, nothing is too difficult for him. The four-wheeler key was half the size of a car key. The head was black, and only the thin part that goes into the ignition was silver. It would be impossible to find. But the girls began to scan the water's edge as their chilled limbs shook uncontrollably. Sarah was sure it had fallen in the water, and she, too, began to cry. The cold river was at least thirty-five feet wide.

Sarah stripped down and retraced their path across the river, wading in up to her waist and looking down at her feet. Then, near a bigger rock, she saw a small shiny flash at an angle. When she stood over it, the rippling water covered it. She didn't know if it was the key, a discarded pop tab, or a lost fishing lure, but she knew it was now or never. Sarah plunged under, blindly reaching around the rocks. It was the first thing she touched. She exploded to the surface, raising the key up in victory.

God was real that day. And I doubt they'll ever forget it.

My older daughter, Katie, also made important connections with God. In the early years of Duncan's sobriety, the atmosphere in our home was volatile. Katie was like an emotional barometer. She felt Duncan's mood swings acutely.

Some days, my husband recognized his sour frame of mind and said, "I'm going upstairs to start my day over." In our bedroom, he turned his troubles over to God, and came down a different man. Katie noticed the change.

Then one day, Katie woke up in a foul mood. She kicked a toy, moaning her frustration over who knows what. After a long moment of silence, she announced, "I'm going upstairs to talk with God and start my day over."

Parenting goes beyond teaching manners and morals. We must bring our children to the threshold of faith. We cannot push or pull them over it. Their crossing is between them and God, exclusively. In the meantime, we have to live by faith, believing that God is at work in unseen ways. And that meantime-faith is pleasing to him.

God also brings us to a greater faith if we tune in to his frequency. He will give us a vision or a promise so we don't lose heart along the way. For example, on the morning of my forty-fourth birthday, I found myself reading Isaiah 44:

> Thus says the Lord who made you and formed you from the womb, who will help you, "Do not fear, O Jacob my servant; and you Jeshurun whom I have chosen. I will pour out My Spirit on your offspring and My blessing on your descendants; and they will spring up among the grass like poplars by streams of water.
>
> *This one will say, "I am the LORD's"; and that one will call on the name of Jacob; and another will write on his hand, "Belonging to the LORD," and will name Israel's name with honor.*[8]

At the time, our daughters were immersed in the dark culture of high school. I had many good reasons to be afraid. Yet God spoke these verses right off the page into my heart. He made a pledge to help his people, and specifically, parents. He promised to pour out his presence and his blessing on the children of Israel. And most interestingly, he referenced three offspring in verse five.

Are you giving me this promise, God? I have three children. I needed a word of hope. Was it just black ink on a thin page or something more? I stared at the phrases, savoring each word. A calm, warm feeling swept over me like a Chinook wind. Closing my eyes, I quieted myself. In my mind's eye, I stood on a pinnacle of revelation as though time had stopped. His words echoed in my mind: *I will help you. Do not fear. I will touch your children.*

Later that day, while cooking dinner, I mindlessly chopped vegetables but my thoughts wandered back to those verses in Isaiah. The voice of doubt whispered in my ear. "Who do you think you are? Those words were for Israel, specifically Jeshurun. You can't claim something like that from God. Your kids have a free will, and their choices could lead them anywhere."

Passively, I agreed with the rebuke. Yes, who was I to think God would say such a big promise to *me*? I sliced more vegetables.

Nate, only seven years old at the time, came bounding into the kitchen, looking for a snack. He sneered when he saw me chopping onions and zucchini. Slumping on the counter, he rested his head on his arms. I glanced over and noticed he had colored something beautiful with Magic Markers on his right hand. "JESUS," it said, in big, bold letters. As a background for the Name-above-all-names, he had sketched a brown, rugged cross with blazing flames.

All chopping ceased. I stared intently at his hand. Shyly, he smiled, happy that I noticed his drawing. *"My God,"* I prayed under my breath.

"What'd you say?" My son turned his face toward me.

But I was captured in a sneeze moment. The words of Isaiah came to life: *another will write on his hand, "Belonging to the Lord."* I took Nate's hand and held it tightly.

My son's puzzled look told me it was my turn to say something. "It's an amazing drawing, Nate." He grinned as I swept him up in my arms, kissing him on the forehead.

God will speak, now one way, then another. When he says something through Scripture and also confirms it in life, you can count on it. God restated Isaiah 44:5, through Magic Marker art, saying, "This is for you, Susan. Hold on to this promise and pray it over your children."

I did and I do. Katie is the one who will say, "I am the Lord's." Over the years, I prayed that her identity would be grounded in God's love—not physical beauty or popularity or attention from boys. God weaned her off these things, redefining her immeasurable worth as his daughter.

Sarah is passionate toward God but wrestling with spiritual questions, as Jacob wrestled the angel of the Lord. But there is a promised ladder, a portal between heaven and earth over her life.

Nate literally wrote the name of Jesus on his hand. The rest of the verse for him remains a mystery, a story yet untold. But one day, I believe I will understand the fullness of these promises with eternal eyes.

Some say God made a terrible mistake when he created human beings and gave them free will. Why would he even consider such a huge gamble? After all, the experiment could go terribly wrong. But God did it anyway, because he wanted relationship.

As parents we take the same chance. In giving birth or adopting a child, we open ourselves up to all the possibilities: everything from glorious joy to unbearable sorrow and every part in between. And why? For the exact same reason.

So who better to travel with than God on this journey called parenting? He more than anyone else understand the risks, the sorrows, and the joys of this holiest of callings.

EIGHTEEN

Three Hammers
Some Thoughts on Prayer

*What seem our worst prayers may really be, in God's eyes,
our best. Those, I mean, which are least supported
by devotional feeling. For these may come from a deeper level
than feeling. God sometimes seems to speak to us
most intimately when he catches us, as it were, off our guard.*
—C. S. LEWIS

Mark Twain was fascinated with Joan of Arc. After many years, he completed a work of fiction entitled *Personal Recollections of Joan of Arc*. In the book he describes a scene in which Joan, an uneducated commoner, spends time with the king of France.

The King was learning to prize her company and value her conversation…he was used to getting nothing out of people's talk but guarded phrases, colorless and non-committal, or carefully tinted to tally with the color of what he said himself; and so this kind of conversation only vexes and bores, and is wearisome; but Joan's talk was fresh and free, sincere and honest, and unmarred by timorous self-watching and constraint. She said the very thing that was in her mind, and said it in a plain, straightforward way.[1]

If an earthly king can relish the authenticity of an ordinary person, how much more does the King of heaven long for us to be our true selves as we pray?

Three years ago, in a Joan kind of way, I laid out my queries and wonderings about prayer. I was amazed that some people could pray for hours, even days. In comparison, I prayed for a little while and ran out of words. Was God more likely to answer longer prayers? How did God feel if I prayed as a discipline but didn't necessarily feel like it? Was it important for my words to be full of passion and desperation? What if I couldn't whip that up? Did God like repetitive prayers or was he bored with continual requests for the same things? These were my questions.

What is it like for God? How does he see our attempts to connect with him? Do you wonder about this too?

Now more developed in my capacity to hear God, I waited with expectancy. The room felt very still. I closed my eyes, hoping to sense God's thoughts on the matter. A few minutes passed. Then, in my mind, I saw three hammers. Like a slideshow, one hammer faded as the next one came into view. I wouldn't have thought of this logically. God sidesteps my mind by handing me a puzzle. In fact, that's one way I know it's him.

First, a doctor's reflex hammer appeared. It was small, with a triangular-shaped rubber head and a metal handle. Next, I saw a judge's wooden gavel, with a cylindrical head. And last, I saw a carpenter's hammer, used to pound nails. The visual pictures were clear but like parables; I needed God's interpretation.

Sometimes God enters the stream of my thoughts as I put pen to paper, so I jotted the images in my journal. The three hammers all served different purposes but somehow represented three distinct ideas about prayer.

A doctor's reflex hammer tests involuntary muscle response. I did some quick research and found that reflexes are triggered by a small nerve pathway between the point of contact and the responding muscle, completely bypassing the brain.[2] I thought about this for a while. In a way, prayer should be a reflex action, like an automatic response to life. It should be something I do almost without thinking, as normal as breathing or swallowing. Prayer isn't limited to certain times, places, disciplines, or formalities. Prayer can be an ongoing, immediate reaction to people and situations around me.

My friend Becky explained this to me a few years ago.

"You know," she said, "prayer is a burden." Surprised by her frankness, I confirmed the sentiment.

"I'll say! I have endless lists of people to pray for. Some days the thought makes me dog tired."

"That's not what I mean," said Becky.

With my elbow on the kitchen table, I rested my chin in my hand.

"The way I see it," she continued, "prayer is a burden *God* puts on your heart."

"Maybe so," I said, "but it still feels *burdensome.*"

"No, no." She shifted her legs and leaned forward on the chair. "I'm not talking about a heavy obligation kind of thing."

"Oh. Okay…" I was suddenly intrigued.

"For instance, sometimes I feel compassion in a situation, or out of the blue, I think about someone who's hurt or in trouble. I think these are moments when God is saying, *Pray about this right now.* He puts a *burden* on me. And when I do, it actually helps me stay in tune with God throughout the day, rather than praying through a list."

I paused, trying to get my mind around her point. *Could it really be that easy?* I measured my prayer life by the clock. She viewed prayer as a frequent tête-à-tête with God. Spontaneous prayer seemed like a great approach.

I decided to give it a try. During the evening news, I listened to the needs and issues going on in the world. I asked God to give wisdom to leaders, protection to soldiers, and comfort to families in tragedy. This felt different, but I liked taking it all to God. When driving around town, I took a moment to pray for homeless and transient people stationed by the exit ramps. As I passed the high school, I prayed for students, teachers, and administrators. When I cooked dinner, worked at the office, or took a walk, I'd pray for any needs God brought to my mind.

When Paul said "pray without ceasing," he gave no timetable, no required number of minutes. Prayer can be continual in the sense of readiness, and God can use anything as a stimulus. It's a drop-what-you're-doing response to life, joining God as he moves in the moment.

One stormy night the phone rang. My friend Maie sounded distraught. Maie and her husband, Gary, lived down the hill from us on Bridger Creek. The stream was rapidly swelling with rainwater. She worried about the overflow coming in and flooding their home. They had moved everything they could upstairs and put heavy furniture and appliances up on blocks. But their house's foundation was vulnerable. We stopped what we were doing and prayed as a family. Our children were young but joined in with simple, sincere phrases.

The next day, Maie called with the news. As it turned out, they had to leave their home in the night. The creek had brimmed over its banks and came up to their floorboards. But when they returned in the daylight, they couldn't believe their eyes.

Two things had saved their house. Upstream from their property sat a huge rock, four to five feet across. Gary thought the boulder weighed well over three-hundred pounds. But in the night, the force of the water carried it downstream, depositing it right by the corner of their house where the current undercut the land. The torrent of water hit the rock instead of the soft soil, preventing what could have been devastating erosion under their home's foundation.

In addition, because the creek surged so quickly, workers were unable to pull the head boards free in the irrigation ditch. The backed-up pressure caused the river to split, diffusing the intensity of the water rushing by their house. Gary and Maie saw the rock and the split river as God's hand of protection. Our family got to experience the miracle with them. Through this and many other examples, I understood the image God gave me. Prayer can be a reflexive response to life's events.

Next I thought about the judge's hammer. In a courtroom, the rap of a gavel signals the pronouncement of a verdict, sealing the division of right from wrong. The Bible says righteousness and justice are the foundation of God's throne.[3] That means God cares about what is right, good, true, and fair. He wants our prayers to reflect those things. When we see injustice, we can pray for justice. If we encounter sickness, we can pray for healing. If someone's spreading lies, we can ask God to reveal the truth.

The problem is, it's easier to grumble than pray. Jesus challenged our tendency toward negativity when he said, "Love your enemies and pray for those who persecute you."[4] God's asking us to turn every pessimistic or critical thought into a prayer for the opposite. When we pray for what God desires—peace, justice, kindness, truth, mercy, humility, repentance, reconciliation—we're asking him to restore order to a disordered world. We become part of the solution.

Think of Abraham pleading with God to spare the city of Sodom. He didn't sit in his comfortable tent thinking, *Oh well, they had it coming.* He asked God to be fair to good people in a bad city. He was concerned for his nephew Lot and Lot's family. Abraham prayed, and God listened and responded.[5] Every time we pray like Abraham did, we're standing in the same heavenly courtroom before the Perfect Judge, asking for what is good, right, true, and fair. The judge's mallet represented this kind of prayer.

The carpenter's hammer was the most straightforward. Every prayer is like pounding a nail into an invisible structure, helping to build a spiritual kingdom. As Scripture says, what is unseen is more real than what is seen.[6]

For example, each time I ask God to protect my children, it's not like he forgot since I last asked him. Rather, every prayer is like a nail, adding strength to a canopy of protection over my kids. Repeated requests are "building" prayers, laying foundations for heaven on earth.

Christianity Today reported an amazing story about the Moravian Christians in the Herrnhut settlement of Saxony (now eastern Germany). In the first five years of its existence, this group of three hundred people showed few signs of spiritual power. By the beginning of 1727, the community was steeped in dissention and bickering. As a solution, leaders agreed to have an around-the-clock prayer watch. A few months later, their society underwent a dramatic transformation following what eyewitnesses called a visitation of the Holy Spirit, similar to the day of Pentecost. Many people were healed and came to faith in God. Miraculous signs and wonders happened with frequency, and unity prevailed. Moravians designate this period as the "golden summer of 1727." The upshot: Herrnhut grew rapidly as the center of a major movement for Christian renewal and missions in the eighteenth century.[7]

One might think a 24/7 prayer meeting for several months is quite a feat. But this prayer vigil continued uninterrupted, 24 hours a day, for *one hundred years*. Other results of prayer from this tiny settlement include the following:

- Publication of *Daily Watchwords* began in 1728 and continues to this day in fifty languages as the oldest and most widely read daily devotional in the world, transcending denominational, political, and racial barriers of all kinds.

- Over thirty settlements have been established globally on the Herrnhut model.

- By 1791 the community had sent three hundred missionaries to all parts of the earth. Over time, the numbers multiplied. Moravians created the first large-scale Protestant missionary movement. They were the first to send unordained lay people, first to go to slaves, and the first in many countries of the world at a time when travel was precarious.

- The group formed many hundreds of small renewal groups, known as diaspora societies, within established churches of Europe, emphasizing personal prayer, worship, Bible study, and accountability.

- Moravians were instrumental in the conversion of John Wesley, founder of the Methodist church and the best-known British leader of the Great Awakening.[8]

All this from a group of three hundred people who were committed to pounding billions of prayer nails, constructing an unseen framework for God's far-reaching purposes then and there—*and* here and now.

Apparently, God likes all kinds of prayer: short prayers said throughout the day *and* marathon prayer vigils. He likes it when we pray as a discipline, even though feelings come and go. God is not bored with repetitive requests but accepts every sincere prayer.

The three hammers gave me a visual picture, rich with meaning. But there are other things I've discovered along the way about communicating with God.

Prayer is spending time with the One I love. I worship him as the Creator when I read Job 37–39 or watch Discovery Channel's *Planet Earth*. Creation is telling the glory of God, and prayer is joining in. This is more than gratitude for things in my life. It's praising him for who he is and what he's like. I've gleaned phrases from Scripture that I pray out loud:

God, you live forever, you have no beginning and no end.
Your name is Holy and you live in a high and holy place.
You also live with the contrite in spirit, and the lowly,
    in order to revive them.
You are the giver of peace to one who is near,
    but also to one who is far away.
We delight in your nearness; when we call, you answer us.
You also go before us; you guard us
    and underneath are your everlasting arms.
Your glory is our rear guard; you surround us with your presence.
You satisfy our scorched places, you give strength to our bones.
You are a healer of the brokenhearted,
    and let us ride on the heights of the earth.

You name every star, and your thoughts
    are more numerous than the sand.
You know when the sparrow falls,
    and the very hairs of our head are counted.
You are able to do exceedingly abundantly
    beyond all that we ask or think.
Many O Lord, are the wonders you have done,
    the earth is full of your glory.

Saying these prayers of praise bring wonder and refreshment.

Another part of prayer is listening for God to speak. Sometimes it's difficult to tune out the din of activity and noise to get quiet. Early mornings work for me, especially when my family is asleep. I often have a journal ready to write down impressions. Sometimes I get a visual image, like the three hammers. Sometimes I hear a phrase or a word that comes like an interruption to my thoughts. Other times, God reminds me of a scripture or words of wisdom from a friend.

I find God speaks more if I meditate on the things he has said.[9] This emphasizes the need to write things down. Often I don't fully understand what God is saying until he intertwines it with other things he's already said or will say later on.

As I learn to recognize God's voice, I believe he looks for my response. God wants doers of his Word, not just hearers.[10] For example, when God puts his finger on gossip in my life, do I resist him, ignore him, or follow through with action? Do I treat him like my alarm clock, hitting the snooze button over and over? I did and I do. To say otherwise would be untrue. But little by little, I've learned obedience is pivotal.

Listening to God is also crucial in times of decision. I love the way David "inquired of the LORD"[11] before acting, even though others, like Saul, plunged ahead with their own ideas and plans. I lived under the mandate of my own agenda for numerous years, doing the Martha thing, not even bothering to talk with God. But when I take time to ask, wait, and listen, usually God will direct my decisions, keep me from overcommitment and confirm his guidance in more than one way.

Prayers are less effectual if there is known sin in my life. For instance, I can't really pray for my husband if my heart is full of resentment.[12] God doesn't like prayers that ask him to "deal" with someone. God checks for humility and resists me when I'm proud or stubborn. He knows if I am motivated by love or by judgment.

God also wants us to be specific in prayer. Sometimes we don't *have,* because we don't ask.[13] I remember driving on a back-country gravel road one January evening,, looking for a shortcut across the valley. With the mountains in view, I wouldn't get totally lost. The car was full of my kids and their friends. Rounding a sharp corner, we blew out a back tire. The car fishtailed slightly, but I managed to pull over. Suddenly, the road seemed very dark and empty. The bitter-cold air invaded the car as I looked for equipment in the storage compartments. Our headlights didn't provide enough light to change the tire, and I didn't have a flashlight. No cell phone either. To make matters worse, the spare tire was chained up under the car. I couldn't see a thing, and the kids were already shivering.

Then my son Nate made an announcement: "I think we should pray." He was only five and the youngest among us, yet he had sized up the problem and found the answer. Admittedly, it wasn't my first thought. Nate prayed boldly, asking God to send someone to help us. Meanwhile, I fumbled around in back, looking for the jack.

Minutes later, headlights came our way. The first and only vehicle we'd seen on this country road stopped. Our good friend Mr. Fremont, returning home from a duck hunt, climbed out of his truck. For some reason, he took this particular back road on his way home. God's timing was impeccable. My son's eyes grew wide. He had asked, and God had answered him. It's easy to see why the kingdom belongs to such as these.

Of course, trusting and allowing God to act according to his own purposes is important. We need to remember God is good, no matter what it looks like. He may not have chosen to send a friend to help us that night. Sometimes he has greater things at stake than the things for which we ask.[14]

But God values sincerity, especially when prayers involve sacrifice. There have been times when I fast and pray long into the night, pressing into him for an answer. Prayers of desperation are powerful.[15] Think of people like Nehemiah who prayed for the deplorable conditions of Jerusalem and God's people there: "When I heard these words, I sat down and wept and mourned for days," he said, "and I was fasting and praying before the God of heaven."[16] And what happened? God gave him favor. The king allowed Nehemiah to repair the city walls, protecting the people from opposition.

Desperate prayers may be the reason so many miracles are happening in places like Africa. My husband travels there extensively to oversee the building and ongoing operations of orphan homes in Uganda where AIDS is rampant.

In August 2003, our family went to visit the projects. One of our orphanage directors had an adult daughter named Josephine who was in the late stages of AIDS. Her death was imminent. Family and friends prepared to take her back to her village for burial, which seemed inevitable. The director asked my husband to pray for her. Others carried Josephine out to the yard where we were greeting the orphans. Though dark-skinned, she looked gray in the sunlight from the debilitating disease.

Duncan and our daughter Katie placed their hands on Josephine's dying body, asking God to heal her in Jesus's name. I stood nearby and joined them silently. I'm sure Josephine's prayers were far more desperate than ours, but together we asked God for a miracle.

Six months later, Josephine e-mailed us:

To: sdhill
Sent: Wednesday, February 11, 2004
Subject: Greetings

Bro. Duncan,

I am strong now. I even have a job as you prayed for me. The
people in my home church are very much interested in you.
They want to see you because of the testimony. And God had
given me part of the anointing you have. I also pray for those
patients who are in the same state as I was and they recover. So
far three people have recovered and they are strong again.... I am
working as a volunteer with a network of people living with
HIV/AIDS. Extend my love to Susan and the children.

Later, Josephine started a microindustry with HIV-positive women
who had lost their husbands. We sell their necklaces in America, and the
proceeds feed the orphans in our homes. Almost five years have passed
since we prayed, and Josephine is still alive and well. This is only one of
countless stories my husband and others have witnessed firsthand. God's
supernatural power manifests on the earth, healing the sick and restoring hope when ordinary people are willing to pray.

Our friend Phil often says, "Communication is an exchange of life."[17]
In the same way, each time we seek out a time, a place, or a moment to
pray, we are in an exchange of life with God. The key word is *exchange*.
Prayer is not a monologue. When we also listen for God's heart and mind,
we will truly come to know the one who said, "My sheep hear My voice,
and I know them, and they follow Me."[18]

Prayer is a simple thing really. You don't have to worry about getting
it just so. With Joan-like openness, you can begin by saying, "Hey God,
it's me. Let's have a talk."

And the King will be all ears.

NINETEEN

A Balding Man in Plaid

Hearing God's Voice for Others

Dwell in possibility.

—EMILY DICKINSON

Years ago Jenny and I met with a woman who was in a great deal of emotional pain. She felt a deep malaise, uncertain if God even cared about her. So we prayed, entreating God to reveal the underlying nature of her anguish.

Scripture says to ask for wisdom from above, because God has insight and knowledge of things we wouldn't humanly know.[1] After praying, we waited. Soon Jenny saw the word *miso* on the screen of her mind. Strange as it was, we didn't think God was talking about soup. We sought out the dictionary, which gave other meanings. Miso is a Greek-derived prefix having to do with hatred. For example, *misogamy* is the hatred of marriage.

The word struck a chord. Yes, the woman admitted, she hated her former husband. He seemed like an entirely different person when they dated. Once married, she felt trapped and betrayed. Tears gathered in her dark brown eyes and spilled down her powdered cheeks. Since her divorce, she'd felt utterly frozen. Hatred had turned her heart to stone. Apparently God was willing to get down to the core problem with one word. Instead of saying "hatred," God gave us a word we wouldn't recognize. It showed her that we weren't just making stuff up. I find that God often speaks in mysteries like this to help us separate our own thinking from his revelation.

Many people spend hours talking to mental health professionals, pouring out their life stories, and that's okay. But I've often seen the Holy Spirit identify core issues quickly, and with great compassion. His wisdom surpasses ours.

Until the woman could come to terms with her bitterness, every new relationship with a man would be poisoned. We discussed her need to grieve her hurts and losses, but at some point she needed to make a choice. She could forgive, shutting the gate on the past to allow an untainted future—or not. Many troubled people either need to forgive or be forgiven, and helping others often centers on this truth.

Soon Jenny and I found ourselves praying for a new person every week and to our amazement, it lasted for years. People came solely on word of mouth. Sessions lasted several hours, but we never took any money. A few people paid our baby-sitters. Sometimes a person's pastor, spouse, or friends came for support. Eventually, we sought guidance and accountability from two pastors.

Jenny and I were just two housewives, desperately interested in what God was doing. We weren't clinically trained counselors. Sometimes we encountered people with multiple personalities, victims of satanic ritual abuse, and others with serious mental disorders. Though we prayed for them, we also referred them to professionals. Even so, many men, women, couples, and children were being touched in profound ways, because God was in the ministry. The apostle Paul said,

> My message and my preaching were not in persuasive words of wisdom, but in *demonstration of the Spirit and of power*, so that your faith would not rest on the wisdom of men, but on the power of God…things we also speak, not in words taught by human wisdom, but in those taught by the Spirit, combining spiritual thoughts with spiritual words." [2]

Our human counsel mattered very little if God didn't display his wisdom and power. As it was, many who came for prayer experienced the reality of God for the first time in their lives.

Early on, the Enemy tried convincing us that we would regret praying for others. Some call this spiritual warfare. The opposition was unmistakable. In the span of one week, all kinds of strange things happened to me. I received an obscene phone call in the middle of the night, which had never happened either before or since. The same caller had phoned Jenny the previous night. A day later, my son came down with hand-foot-and-mouth disease, and my husband got an eye infection. Next, our septic system backed up and sewage ruined the downstairs carpet. Then, while taking a walk in my neighborhood, two men followed me in a truck, making rude, salacious comments. I ran home and quickly locked the door, my heart wildly pounding.

Lord, these attacks are all so bizarre. What's happening here? I sat on the three steps leading to the kitchen and opened my Bible. God's Word often brings solace. Still trembling, I was turning to Psalms but stopped in Isaiah. I wasn't expecting such a direct message:

> I, even I, am He who comforts you. Who are you that you are afraid of man who dies, and of the son of man who is made like grass; that you have forgotten the LORD your Maker, who stretched out the heavens and laid the foundations of the earth; that you fear continually all day long because of the fury of the oppressor, as he makes ready to destroy? But where is the fury of the oppressor?
>
> The exile will soon be set free, and will not die in the dungeon, nor will his bread be lacking.
>
> For I am the LORD your God, who stirs up the sea and its waves roar (the LORD of hosts is His name).
>
> And I have put My words in your mouth, and have covered you with the shadow of My hand, to establish the heavens, to found the earth, and to say to Zion, "You are My people." [3]

You can't believe how those verses affected me. He spoke the words right off the page, addressing all my concerns with specific phrases. Yes, I was afraid. The Enemy's fury was real, and I had forgotten the mighty power of God. The Lord would cover me with protection.

He also spoke about setting captives free. Loads of people are trapped in dungeons of fear, hate, sin, pride, and many other forms of bondage. Our prayers for those people mattered. God confirmed that he would give us his words, his knowledge, and his wisdom. I calmed down, resting in the wonder of a God who would answer me so unequivocally.

As we continued praying for others, taking notes became my primary role. I wasn't as experienced as Jenny in hearing the Lord, so I held back, fearing presumption. Occasionally she asked, "Are you getting anything?" I would just shake my head.

Awhile later, our pastor friend Jack came down from Whitefish to teach on the subject of hearing God's voice. First, he said, it's necessary to scrutinize any extrabiblical revelation in the clear light of Scripture. In other words, God's fresh words will not contradict his written Word. So knowing the Bible was imperative. No shortcuts there.

He also explained that hearing God involved three components: revelation, interpretation, and application. When Jenny had heard the word *miso,* that was revelation. Sometimes God speaks plainly, but more often it's in puzzles and mysteries, leaving room for faith. Interpretation is a critical link. When we discovered that *miso* meant "hatred," it made sense to the woman. She described her deep-seated anger, and we talked about the need for forgiveness. If she agreed to apply God's principles of forgiveness, her life could change. It was all about what God revealed, what it meant, and what to do with it.

Jack said that the likelihood of mishandling God's voice centered on interpretation and application. I thought of Paul admonishing the Galatians, saying, "You who are spiritual, restore [others] in a spirit of gentleness...for if anyone thinks he is something when he is nothing, he deceives himself."[4] A simple guideline we used proved to be a useful safeguard:

We often asked the person for *his or her* interpretation saying, "Does that mean anything to you?" And we only talked about application if we sensed a willing heart.

Jack closed the seminar with prayer, asking God to give us a revelation for someone else in the room. I thought, *Well, okay,* and shut my eyes and waited. My mind was empty like television static at the end of a broadcast day. I squinted hard and really tried to see or hear anything, anything at all. Nothing. So I gave up and let my mind wander, daydreaming the time away.

Before I knew it, I saw in my mind's eye a balding man in a plaid shirt. I saw his face from the side as if I were looking over his shoulder. His expression seemed heavy with great sorrow. Gradually, a bright light from above made his face glow. He looked up and smiled, as if something wonderful was happening to him.

That was it.

Jack asked the audience of several hundred people whether anyone had received some kind of impression from God. I kept my hand down as several people raised theirs and scanned the audience for a balding man in a plaid shirt. I didn't see anyone. Three people responded to Jack's question.

Not much time left, I thought. Maybe I'd get out of it. I didn't want to look foolish. But I'd seen something, even if it didn't mean anything.

Okay, God. If Jack asks for one more example, I'll do it.

Wouldn't you know it? He did. I swallowed hard and awkwardly rose from my seat. Why was this so difficult? But I fought through it, sharing the image of the balding man. Jack looked around the crowd.

"Is there anyone here that fits this description?"

A dozen rows directly in front of me, a man slowly stood up. His hair was receding and he wore a plaid shirt. I suddenly felt plugged into an electrical current, buzzing with anticipation and fear.

Oh no! What now?

Jack turned to me and said, "What do you think your impression means?"

I fumbled for words. "Well, I think the man I saw in my mind's eye seemed deeply troubled. But maybe the light was God. Perhaps his expression changed because, well maybe God would give him understanding and hope." I sounded tentative, but Jack asked the man if this applied to his situation. The man nodded.

Jack motioned me to come up and quietly pray for this hurting man. Still buzzing, I walked stiffly up the aisle as four other men popped out of their seats to join me. Evidently, they were friends of the man in plaid. One man was his pastor.

I asked the man how I could pray for him. His eyes were moist and half-closed with heaviness. Grief weighed on his shoulders like sandbags. He told me his father had been diagnosed with a very aggressive brain tumor, and another family member had just died. The other men seemed to know these details already. I reached for his hands, even though mine were sweaty and quivering. Together we surrounded him with prayer, asking God to shower his light on all the trouble, giving this man hope for the days ahead.

I returned to my seat, utterly stunned and still shaking inside. What had just happened? What if I had been a coward? That man would have missed a blessing. Instead, he left the seminar feeling known and loved by the King of heaven.

If his friends had given him an impression like that, it wouldn't have been the same. They knew the details of his pain. God's encouragement for him came from a perfect stranger, and that's exactly why he knew it was from God.

Recently, I contacted this man to confirm the story for the book. He e-mailed me saying:

> Yes, we sure remember you and Duncan. As I recall, the conference was in mid- or late January. That was a very significant event for me. My father was dying at the time. In November he had been diagnosed…and by mid-February he died. One of my

uncles had just died, and my great-aunt (with whom I was very close) was also failing and ended up dying a few months later. No question, it was a very difficult time for me and my family.

I remember how difficult it was for me to go to the conference instead of spending that extra time with Dad, but I felt very strongly about going. Certainly God honored that decision by blessing and encouraging me and you…and lots of other people too. I'd taken a friend with me. We were sitting together when you spoke. He looked at me and cringed and said, "Oh man, it's you dude, it's you." I know he was very touched by what happened. Also my wife reminded me how much she and our kids were blessed when I came home so encouraged that night, as we were all going through those difficult times.

Pastor Jack ended the meeting saying that sometimes you don't know if an impression, a word, or a phrase is from God until you act on it, stepping out in faith. He cautioned us, however—in hearing God's heart for others, we should exercise utmost humility and guard against presumption.

Hearing God definitely involves a learning curve. Some initial impressions were probably my own imagination, though God influenced them in some measure. But over time the ratio shifted. With practice I gradually noticed a difference, just like one can learn the nuances of a new language. However, if you reject the whole idea and never start the process, you will miss a breathtaking dimension of the Christian life.

As I grew in my ability to hear God, I was asked to join the ministry/prayer team at my church. After Sunday morning services, Pastor David frequently invited people who needed prayer, to come to the front of the church sanctuary. Usually I spoke all-purpose prayers for them and waited on God for discernment.

One time a man in his twenties came forward. I'll call him Joel. When I asked about his prayer needs, he mumbled a few things about stress at school and going home for Christmas. As counselors know, time and again, the "presenting problem" isn't the real problem. I honored his requests, but inside, I sought wisdom. *What do you see, Lord? What do you know?*

Immediately, in my mind's eye I saw a bucket with a wash rag draping over its edge. Gently I asked Joel if he felt unclean before God. He nodded but gave me a look of surprise. His emotions were stirred. I didn't dig for specifics, although now I knew how to pray. I asked God to set Joel free from condemnation. A tear dropped on his shirt. I prayed for God to meet him in his struggles. And finally, I asked God to increase all the ways he spoke to Joel, so he would know God is real, that he cares, and no matter what, that God is for him, not against him. By then, the young man's torso shook with sobs.

God knew exactly how to connect with him. Humanly speaking, I didn't. I could have prayed nice prayers for God to help him with school and his trip home, but it would have been superficial. God's love poured out of heaven, depositing intimacy directly into Joel's heart.

As you have probably noticed by now, in most situations I'm a cautious person. I hold back, afraid to appear silly or, worse, meddling. Still, I learned the hard way that not all bits of revelation are for sharing. Some things are simply a matter for prayer. For example, I had a striking dream about a certain man I knew and his teenage son.

In the dream, the father decides the son needs to learn a lesson. He punishes him by turning his son's long lanky body upside down in a utility sink to wash his mouth out with soap. Though just an observer, I could feel the son's humiliation. It's degrading to be treated as a child when you're nearing adulthood. The father seems oblivious to his son's feelings. He thinks punishing his son is the right thing to do. Afterward, the son kneels on the ground, his expression heavy with dejection. Slowly, he looks up at his father with piercing hatred in his eyes. Then the entire scene splits down the middle with the son on the left and the father on right. Unresolved bitterness divides them and brings alienation.

Clearly, it was a warning dream. God in his kindness cautioned many people through dreams in the Bible. An angel came to Joseph in a dream, instructing him not to leave his fiancée, Mary, though her pregnancy appeared disgraceful.[5] God warned the Pharaoh about seven years of famine through a dream about seven cows.[6] I knew God sent warning dreams.

Though a small percentage of my dreams are for others, I also thought of verses in which God challenged his people to warn others:

If the watchman sees the sword coming and does not blow the
trumpet and the people are not warned, and a sword comes and
takes a person from them, he is taken away in his iniquity; but
his blood I will require from the watchman's hand.[7]

But I didn't pause and ask God what to do. I typed up a synopsis and sent it off to the father. The dream had clear images and a story line. I didn't go to bed trying to make something up. I didn't write my opinion on parenting styles or counsel the man in any way. I just wrote down the raw material, leaving the interpretation and the application to the Holy Spirit. Unfortunately, the man was acutely offended. To this day, I wonder if I did the right thing in sending him the dream. Maybe God just wanted me to pray.

Yet dreams aren't always a judgment, saying, "This will happen." Like many biblical prophecies, dreams can also be conditional. A big question mark is attached to the outcome, leaving room for a different conclusion based on our response. God's kindness is embedded in warning dreams, like when we tell our children to look both ways before crossing the street.

In other circumstances, timing is the issue. For instance, I had a dream about my friend Alissa. In the dream, Alissa and I are talking in her driveway on a beautiful summer day. A kind man stands next to me, though I never see his face. I tell Alissa what a wonderful husband she has, describing how hard working, respectful, and thoughtful he is. Alissa slowly shakes her head. Though she conceals her thoughts with careful words, her disappointment is evident. Then the man standing with us speaks up: "You know, even the best of men cannot weather deep anger." The dream ended there.

I knew that in real life, Alissa had been intensely hurt in a previous marriage. Her first husband violated their vows through infidelity and left her to raise their son alone. She moved across the country, running from the pain. Along the highway, she saw the word *Jesus* tacked up on fence posts, trees, and billboards. She felt God was with her, but her heart was still broken.

Now she's married to a good man. The dream prompted me to pray for them as a couple, but I didn't share the story with her. After my previous experience with the father-son dream, I played it safe.

For some reason, however, God would not let me forget the dream. Months later, I saw glimpses of the same driveway scene. For instance, a TV commercial showed a woman making disparaging remarks about her husband to another woman. Then, in church, a woman whispered negative comments about her husband to me. Again, I remembered the dream about Alissa. Was this God's reflex hammer tapping me to pray? Or did God want more? Was he prompting me to tell Alissa the dream?

As time went on, I sensed he wanted me to tell her. *Okay, okay, God. I'll call her up!* I phoned her at work and told her the whole dream in thirty seconds.

"Okay," she said. "Thanks. Gotta go. Bye." And that was that. Or so I thought.

A few weeks later, she called my cell.

"Hey Susan, remember that dream you had? You know, where we talked in my driveway?"

"Uh, I guess so." Of course I remembered. My heart rate accelerated.

"Well, it started a chain reaction."

Oh boy, I thought. *Now I'm in trouble.*

"I've been going to counseling for a while, because I'm still getting over all the hurt from my first marriage."

I shifted the phone to my right ear. "I see."

"Anyway, I told your dream to the counselor, and she was amazed. She had tried bringing up the subject of anger in our meetings for a long time but felt I was too angry to talk about it!" She let out a big laugh.

I chuckled nervously. "So what happened?"

"Well, she gave me this article on anger, and honestly, it fits. I've stuffed my feelings for so long, trying to make everything okay, but it's just not okay. Your dream opened up the discussion."

"That's so grea—"

"But wait, you won't believe this. The very next Sunday, my husband and I were sitting in church, and guess what? The pastor's sermon was all about anger. He said if you don't resolve the pain from a failed marriage, it can greatly damage or destroy your next one. Can you believe that?"

By now you'd think I could, wouldn't you? But I stood there shaking my head, marveling at God's perfect timing. Now we both understood the mysterious words of the kind man in the dream.

Each time we hear the voice of the Lord for others, we're not just passing on information, as vital as that may be. We're demonstrating that God is real and knows each of us individually. We contradict the notion of an impersonal God out in the universe, swirling in some vast cloud of energy, oblivious to the human struggle. God is here and now, a present help in trouble.

Time and again, Jenny and I saw the reality of what Paul described in 1 Corinthians 14:25. He was talking about the gift of prophecy. When God supernaturally gives us something for another, "the secrets of his heart are disclosed; and so he will fall on his face and worship God, declaring that God is certainly among you."

One such person I will treasure forever.

Jenny and I met with a man named Dimitri one afternoon. His friend came along for support. We pulled some chairs close to a futon couch

Jenny had in her basement. They had traveled a long way, and Dimitri seemed tired and weak.

You see, he was dying of AIDS.

We held hands and began to pray, asking for God's protection and wisdom. A period of listening and waiting followed. God revealed themes of abandonment, fear, sorrow, rejection, and misunderstanding that had dominated Dimitri most of his life. Jenny heard the phrase "utter destruction of the soul." I remember feeling alarmed and exchanged glances with Jenny. Dimitri was a deeply wounded man.

As we discussed those themes with Dimitri, his story unfolded. As a child he experienced some of the worst physical and emotional abuse. Alcoholism and witchcraft played roles. He wasn't allowed to have a mind of his own, and he didn't feel acknowledged as a person. He was made to feel inferior to his siblings because his skin color was darker than theirs. The only love he experienced came from his grandfather, who died when Dimitri was only seven or eight years old. The loss was devastating. At the age of fourteen, Dimitri ran away from everything familiar to start a new life.

Many details came to light as we listened and prayed. After a while, Jenny began to hear a series of short phrases. She spoke them slowly and directly to Dimitri, one after another. I had time to write it all down:

My son,

My heart is moved with compassion for you. You have been imprisoned most of your life. The angels have wept at the things that have been done to you. How many times I have longed to intercede, to sweep you up off the earth and bring you home. But your life has been for a purpose, and it is not yet time.

There has been much evil arrayed against you. But you can be set free. I have brought you to this day for that purpose, but you must choose me. You must choose me, for I have chosen you.

At this point, Dimitri said out loud, "I choose you, Lord Jesus." All of us were weeping. Crumpled tissues piled up everywhere. I kept wiping my eyes in order to write. Tears flood my eyes even now as I remember that afternoon—the presence of God all around us, and the compassion of his voice. The phrases continued:

> Only I can fulfill the desire in you that is so deep, that is lonely, that is so sad and filled with sorrow. No person can fill that space, my son, for it was created for me. You are surrounded by hardness and bitterness and pain and hurt. How I want to tear down those walls. I long to hear you say that I am yours and you are mine. Let me move in your life. Let me heal the wounds. Let me heal the sorrow.
>
> My son, you have been running from pain all your life. You have had a piece taken out of your soul by all the pain. Trust in me, and I will restore that. My love is for you, my son. It is for you.
>
> *Raoul*, do not be afraid...

Startled, Jenny stopped and looked up. She asked Dimitri if he went by a different name. He was completely speechless for a moment. Pain-filled emotions choked his voice. Finally, he looked at her through tearful eyes and spoke. Raoul was his real name. When he ran away, he changed his name as a way of breaking ties with everything and everyone who had hurt him. Humanly, Jenny didn't know this. But God knew the secrets of his heart and called him by name.

Dimitri opened up his life to God that very afternoon. It wasn't because we had persuasive arguments about Christianity. It wasn't because we were expert psychologists. He crossed the threshold of faith because God demonstrated his power and love through everyday people.

Jesus told the Samaritan woman at the well that she had had five husbands and was presently with a man who was not her husband. He spoke without condemnation. He offered her living water so she would never thirst again. She dropped her water pots and ran to the city, saying, "Come, see a man who told me all the things that I have done; this is not the Christ, is it?"[8]

When God reveals that he sees, hears, and knows all about us and offers his love anyway, who can resist? Many fall in love with Jesus and never get over it.

That would be me. And I hope it is you.

Hearing God for yourself is essential. Hearing God for others must be done with great care, with biblical context and accountability to others, as my next chapter will discuss in detail.

But you shouldn't believe me. You need to investigate this for yourself. You must determine if you want to be in the great outpouring of God's Spirit as promised in the book of Joel and reiterated in the book of Acts:

> "And it shall be in the last days," God says, "That I will pour forth of My Spirit on all mankind; and your sons and your daughters shall prophesy, and your young men shall see visions, and your old men shall dream dreams; even on my bondslaves, both men and women, I will in those days pour forth of My Spirit and they shall prophesy."[9]

How many people today have never experienced God's love like the Samaritan woman at the well? At the time, she had a mixed-up theology and a lifetime of mistakes. Jesus knew all that. But the supernatural love of God changed everything in a moment.

For that matter, how many people are sitting in church with correct theology and exemplary lives but with faith that feels hollow because they've never experienced a personal encounter with God?

With the Holy Spirit's help, we *can* follow Jesus's example, freely giving his love, his supernatural knowledge, and his living water to others. It still requires faith. But if we will join God in this venture, he will increase our understanding of just how deep and high, far and wide is the expansive love of Christ.

TWENTY

Psychic Christians?

A Word on Presumption

*Beloved, do not believe every spirit, but test the spirits
to see whether they are from God; because many false prophets
have gone out into the world.*

—JOHN THE APOSTLE, 1 JOHN 4:1

I n May 1995 author Rebecca Lee wrote a piece called "The Jerusalem Syndrome" for *The Atlantic Monthly*. She describes how each year a number of visitors to Jerusalem "snap under the historical and religious weight of the city and begin to believe that they themselves are the Messiah or the Virgin or King David or, more commonly, God or Satan." The syndrome has been around for centuries, even going back to Peter the Hermit, a leader of the early Crusades. Since then, Jerusalem has seen "a long line of pilgrims who have abandoned their own identities in search of divinity."

Lee wrote that locals are well acquainted with this phenomenon. Preliminary symptoms may include falling behind in the tour group or becoming irritated with traveling companions. Eventually there's preaching or excessive singing, and some end up walking around in bed sheets. Though the condition is not regarded as a true psychosis, many are taken to a psychiatric hospital called Kfar Shaul, which specializes in this affliction.

Yair Bar El, head of the hospital, named the Jerusalem Syndrome in 1982 and sees those afflicted as "religious casualties—people who got too close to the fire and caught fire themselves." He treats people on a case-by-case basis: a woman who is pregnant with God's child but unable to give birth until the world is reformed, or a "Jesus" who contacts the Israeli police to turn in unbelievers. Once Bar El put two "messiahs" in a room and asked them to determine which one was the imposter. More than an hour later, they both still claimed to be the true Messiah.

An overwhelming majority of the cases involve people with psychological or behavioral problems, according to Eliezer Witztum, professor of psychiatry at the Negev Faculty of Health Sciences at the Mental Health Center in Beersheva. What's interesting, however, is that 18 percent of the victims are ordinary people who come to visit Jerusalem. Of this group, most believe for a few days to a week that they are someone of biblical notoriety. Lee calls it a "brief divine intoxication."

She mentions several of these "normal" victims in her article: a kindergarten teacher comes to Jerusalem and believes she is pregnant with the new Savior. Returning home to her husband in Maine, she never says anything about it. An American pastor stands at Golgotha and feels an intense conviction that he is the Messiah returning to the earth. Five days later he flies home and speaks as usual in his pulpit. Only his wife worries about his temporary divine confusion.

The most well-known case in our country was David Koresh, who recognized his supposed divinity on a trip to Jerusalem in 1983. Lee suggests that if he had been treated at Kfar Shaul and given haloperidol, a dopamine-controlling drug, the Waco tragedy could have been averted.[1]

Authorities may relegate the syndrome to psychological terms, but there's a definite spiritual dimension to this anomaly if you believe the Bible's stance on demonic activity. Demons can and do influence people's minds. Why else would Jesus put a demon-possessed person back in his "right mind"?[2]

One could dismiss the phenomenon, saying, "Well, weird things happen in a city with all that religious history." But delusion and demonic oppression go hand in hand and can happen anywhere.

Closer to home, in a small midwestern town, there lived a faithful, churchgoing family. At least initially, they appeared so. The father, whom I will call Bill, read the Bible and felt called to be a missionary. He was always in the church working with the pastor. But as time passed, he moved his family to a remote location, isolating them from their community and church. Then one day, he caught his wife in a white lie. A fight between them escalated, and he shot her. Though she survived the assault, she divorced her husband while he sat in prison. Their children, now adults, are still reeling from the trauma.

The real story came from people who knew them very well. Warning signs were abundant. Friends said that Bill viewed himself as a prophet and was frequently at the church to "help" the pastor. He acted spiritually superior toward those in authority. He twisted truth, passing judgment on people instead of encouraging them. Over time, he went from a show-no-mercy legalism with others to a "cheap grace" mentality for himself: "I can do anything, and God will forgive me." Some who conversed with him felt baited into a trap. He'd talk in circles, saying they were wrong because they didn't have the whole truth. He was physically, sexually, and emotionally abusive to his wife but had a following of women in the church. And if his children disobeyed him, he threatened them with an Old Testament stoning.

The pastor and others began to challenge and confront Bill, so he moved his family into seclusion to avoid accountability. He manhandled his wife and children with intimidation and control. His extreme behavior worsened and tension increased. When he shot his wife, the nightmare finally ended.

Stories like these are rare, but most of us have heard a few of them or even experienced something like it in our churches, communities, or families. Presumption and deception are real. Reports on the news range from abortion-clinic bombers to Christians protesting homosexuality at military funerals. These incidents, in turn, fuel a smear campaign against Christians who say, "God told me to." In some circles, Christians are the butt of the joke, not the light of world.

The problem is not limited to one crazed individual. Jeffrey Lundgren and about two dozen followers splintered off the mainstream Church of Jesus Christ of Latter-day Saints to form what most would call a cult. He said, "It's not a figment of my imagination that I can in fact talk to God.... I am a prophet of God. I am even more than a prophet."[3] Arrested for murder, he said in his defense that God had ordered him, through interpretation of scriptures (maybe Acts 5:1–11), to kill the Avery family for their lack of faith. He believed the Averys were disloyal to God for not pooling their money into the church fund. Lundgren's last words were, "I'd like to profess my love for God, my family, my children, and my beloved wife. ... I am because you are."[4]

Karen, the youngest Avery, was only seven.

In the previous story, everyone knew that the man who shot his wife was deluded. But what's really scary in the Lundgren case is that other cult members also believed the cold-blooded murders were okay with God. These people were ordinary, middle-class, Bible-reading Americans.

In a post 9/11 world, we know spiritual delusion isn't limited to one group or religion. It's a human problem. Everyone is susceptible to the Father of Lies. On the matter of hearing God's voice today, this presents a clear danger.

So how do we reconcile this reality with a God who explicitly said, "My sheep hear My voice"?[5] "I have many more things to say to you," Jesus said, "but you cannot bear them now. But when He, the Spirit of truth, comes, He will guide you into all the truth; for He will not speak on His own initiative, but whatever He hears, He will speak; and He will disclose to you what is to come."[6]

Unable to resolve this dilemma, many Christians end up with a play-it-safe spirituality. Apprehensive about anything supernatural, they prefer a staid Christianity, having all of the form but little of the power. Some have tidied up church history books, editing out everything from peculiar incidents to phenomenal miracles. Countless believers are taught that God only speaks through his written Word, even though the Word itself says God speaks through dreams, visions, circumstances, impressions, and even an audible voice.

For instance, Peter's trancelike vision of a sheet filled with animals, birds, and creatures of all kinds came with a voice that said, "Get up, Peter, kill and eat!" [7] Amazingly, the early church accepted this vision as proof that God desired the inclusion of Gentiles in his kingdom—a gigantic shift in Jewish thinking. In today's climate of rigorous skepticism, would anyone accept such a doctrinal change based on a strange symbolic vision? Not a chance. We would say Peter was a flake, a fanatic, and at the very least, delusional. Yet the book of Acts is full of the Holy Spirit speaking and moving among God's followers, building the church in supernatural ways.

When Jenny and I worked in prayer ministry, we heard rumors that some people called us psychic Christians. From what I could tell, it sounded like a compliment, similar to the Samaritan woman's response, "Come and see—there's a God who knows me!" Of course, we didn't put up a sign using this term. Psychics are not receiving their information from God. Still, the term showed how deeply people long for an authentic experience with God.

On the other hand, those who called us psychic Christians may have assumed we were dabbling in dark realms. Let's face it—hearing God in real time isn't exactly mainstream...yet. Some Christians believe the Enemy's power to deceive them is greater than God's desire to speak today in a book-of-Acts kind of way. So they tune out the possibilities, fearing anything remotely paranormal.

Yet the postmodern world is desperately searching for the supernatural. Secular thinkers and younger generations, in particular, have gone beyond believing that science, education, politics, or technology will fix our Humpty-Dumpty brokenness—but they're looking for God in all the wrong places.

There are only two kinds of supernatural power: the good and the bad. And the bad doesn't necessarily look ugly. The Enemy is very successful at appearing as an angel of light. For example, I saw a bumper sticker recently that said, "Witches heal." That is true, but people don't understand that healing from the wrong source comes with bondage. Many good people are stumbling into the bad supernatural because it looks good, and the church has not filled a void in their lives. Entrenched in unbelief, we are not exercising the spiritual gifts as explained by Paul in 1 Corinthians 12, and therefore, we're not growing in discernment. Out of fear, we resort to rhetoric about God but fail to show our searching world his power.

Hearing God should be normal Christianity.

But how can we guard ourselves from presumption, deception, and delusion, especially while we're on the steep part of the learning curve? How do we know if we're really hearing God?

First, judge by the fruit. A Pharisee named Gamaliel was a respected teacher of the Law. In some ways he represents the good Christian of today. Gamaliel undoubtedly heard of the miraculous signs and wonders surrounding Peter and the other disciples. But the supernatural makes religious people uncomfortable, and the Council of Pharisees wanted to put an end to it. Gamaliel basically advised his peers to judge people and miraculous events by what came of them:

> Men of Israel, take care what you propose to do with these men.
> For some time ago Theudas rose up, claiming to be somebody,
> and a group of about four hundred men joined up with him.

But he was killed, and all who followed him were dispersed and came to nothing.

After this man, Judas of Galilee rose up in the days of the census and drew away some people after him; he too perished, and all those who followed him were scattered. So in this present case, I say to you…if this plan or action is of men, it will be overthrown; but if it is of God, you will not be able to overthrow them; or else you may even be found fighting against God.[8]

In fact, Jesus said much the same thing. When John the Baptist was imprisoned by Herod, he sent his disciples to ask Jesus if he was the one they were expecting. His answer was telling: "Go and report to John what you hear and see: the blind receive sight and the lame walk, the lepers are cleansed and the deaf hear, the dead are raised up, and the poor have the gospel preached to them."[9] Jesus asked them to judge him by what he did, not by what he claimed to be.

Earlier he said to the multitudes, "Beware of the false prophets, who come to you in sheep's clothing, but inwardly are ravenous wolves. You will know them by their fruits. Grapes are not gathered from thorn bushes nor figs from thistles, are they?…So then, you will know them by their fruits."[10]

It may take awhile to know what's ripening, but eventually, the truth comes out. Hearing God should make us closer to God, more loving toward people, ready to bless, build up, and edify the church—and more important, those outside the church. Hearing God shouldn't lead to self-aggrandizement, manipulation of others, or actions that harm or deceive.

Second, an important safeguard against presumption and deception is a willingness to remain under authority. When Jenny and I prayed for others, we were advised by two pastors. If we said or did anything inappropriate or flat-out wrong, we wanted correction. But even if we only heard God's voice for ourselves, the same principle applied. In Bill's case, his lack of respect for authority was the first warning sign.

Third, the Bible is our source. What God said in Scripture through his prophets, apostles, and others gives context for anything he might say today. God speaks in the foundational language of biblical truth, but he builds on that bedrock. He takes these truths and reiterates them in a personal vernacular that is fresh, poignant, and timely to the individual. Whether he speaks through a circumstance, a dream, or the still small voice, he is always consistent with his written Word. I'm leery of people who say they hear from God but don't know their Bible. It's too easy to make God what you want him to be, instead of *who he is.* Studying the Bible and being taught by leaders with Biblical training should go hand in hand with learning to hear God's fresh voice.

Also, the sum of God's Word is his truth. As we read verses, we should become adept at balancing Scripture with other scriptures. Perhaps Lundgren used the story of Ananias and Sapphira in Acts 5 as biblical justification to kill followers who didn't give all their money to the church. If so, he failed to notice that God, not Peter, took their lives. Maybe Lundgren never read that Jesus saved the woman caught in adultery from being stoned.[11] Or when Jesus was not received in Samaria, James and John said, "Lord, do You want us to command fire to come down from heaven and consume them?" But Jesus rebuked them, saying, "You do not know what kind of spirit you are of; for the Son of Man did not come to destroy men's lives, but to save them."[12] Knowing the Bible doesn't mean simply quoting isolated verses. It's imperative to read and compare many verses. Our goal should be to understand the whole Bible.

We must also reference the Bible's symbolic language when interpreting dreams, visions, and mental impressions, instead of relying on pop psychology. The Bible gives meaning to numbers, colors, objects, and much more. Excellent resources for Bible-based dream interpretation are available. (See suggested resources in the reading guide.)

God can give dreams to warn us, to give guidance, to teach, to instill hope, or to stir our prayers. Consider some of the many remarkable things that have happened in history because of dreams. Julius Caesar's death was foretold in his wife's dream. In 312 AD, Constantine had a dream about Jesus on the cross. As a result, he mandated tolerance for Christians through the Edict of Milan in 313 AD. St. Francis of Assisi also saw Jesus on the cross in a dream. Jesus told him to "Go set my house in order," and thus, St. Francis founded the Franciscan order. Einstein's theory of relativity came from his dreams, and George Frideric Handel wrote *Messiah* after he heard it in a dream.[13]

But not all dreams are from God. Some dreams are merely wishful thinking or carnal desires on the night screen of our minds. Yet, to say dreams are too subjective a means for God to use to speak today is contrary to the Bible itself.

Finally, fellowship is all important. The Enemy zeros in on the lone ranger. Spiritually mature believers can guide us as we learn to recognize what is God's voice and what isn't. We also discover more about hearing God through others' stories. Most important, in relationship we find accountability.

Understanding the role of authority, growing in biblical understanding, and receiving guidance and accountability through fellow believers are key safeguards. But there are other ways God protects us too.

Remember, God often confirms his thoughts in more than one way. If God impresses on a man that a certain woman will be his wife, the wrong response would be to run out, buy a ring, and propose. Another wrong response would be to say, "That could never happen." If the man truly heard from the Lord, God would confirm it in other ways, particularly to the woman who would be his wife.

Another safeguard is to learn to recognize counterfeits. As demonstrated in the story of Moses and the plagues, when God sent frogs to cover the land, the Pharaoh's magicians did the same with their secret arts.[14]

It may have been hard for some to discern who was more powerful, until God's miracles outmatched the magicians.

On the surface, the good and the bad supernatural can often seem the same. For instance, while astronomy isn't supernatural, it's a valid science pointing to the vastness of creation and the concept of infinity. Space in its very existence is evidence of God's supernatural power. Yet the Enemy has turned the study of stars into fortune-telling through astrology. People make deductions and predictions based on planets and stars in relation to human events. Horoscopes are the most prevalent form. If you're not getting supernatural information from God, you're getting it from the Enemy, and this is called divination.

According to *The New Unger's Bible Dictionary, divination* is "the art of obtaining knowledge, especially of the future. Divination comes from demonic power, whereas genuine prophecy is from the Spirit of God."[15] Seeking knowledge from any source other than God opens a door to the Enemy in your life. You might as well put out a welcome mat.

Or consider the significance of numbers in the Bible compared with the occult practice of numerology. Numbers are part of the Bible's symbolic language. For instance, God numbers the stars in the sky and the hairs on our heads. The number 50 is the year of jubilee and freedom in Jewish culture; 666 is the number of the Antichrist.

But numerology teaches people to place faith in numerical patterns instead of God. It's fortune-telling and divination in yet another package. Numerology has been around for a long time; it was popular with early mathematicians, such as Pythagoras.[16] Some use numerology in stock market analysis. One recent movie, *The Number 23,* depicts a man obsessed with a book about the number 23. He sees that the number patterns in his real life coincide with the character in the book, and all of them add up to the number 23. The book ends with a murder. The man fears that the book has foretold his destiny, trapping him in a curse he can't undo.[17]

Yet God speaks through numbers. When I saw 7:10 on the coffee-maker clock, he was reminding me of a special scripture. When I wrote about twenty-eight stones completing a pattern for an eternity ring, I described a symbolic word from God that was based on other encouragement he gave for my marriage. My faith is in God, not the numbers.

Sometimes I open my Bible or a devotional, and God speaks something relevant to me right from that page. But to test God by closing my eyes, randomly opening the Bible and pointing to a verse is akin to using the Bible like a Magic 8-Ball. Is has to do with your intention. Do you see the distinction? Clearly, as we grow in hearing God's voice, we must also grow in discernment.

What's most disturbing to me is the dichotomy I see among believers today: On one hand, there are biblically grounded Christians who resist God's fresh voice altogether out of fear and unbelief. On the other end of the spectrum, I find Christians who are open to the supernatural ways of God but undiscerning about the Enemy's imitations and who don't know their Bibles. The first group accuses the second of being deceived. The second accuses the first of limiting God. But we all are unprepared if we don't know both the Bible and the Holy Spirit.

Safeguards are important considerations, but undoubtedly the best protection against presumption and deception is not just identifying the counterfeits. It's far better to know the real thing: a God who spoke in the Bible yet still speaks today.

For so many years my spiritual growth was limited to another page of notes in my notebook. Pretty two-dimensional, if you ask me. But as my longing for a multidimensional God increased, I stepped out of the safe confines of human religiosity. God was drawing me with lovingkindess into a relationship, and I learned to remain grounded in the process. And in my view, it was entirely worth the risk.

TWENTY-ONE

Beloved
You're God's Favorite, and So Am I

The LORD appeared to him from afar, saying, "I have loved you with a everlasting love; therefore I have drawn you with lovingkindness."

—JEREMIAH 31:3 (NASB)

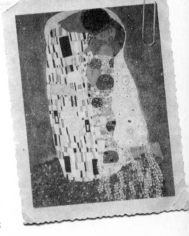

met Stacey at a writers conference. He wore dark-rimmed glasses and had a friendly smile. I guessed he was in his late twenties or early thirties. He looked at me with familiarity, though I had never seen him before. We exchanged the basic information: where we were from, why we were here, what we were writing. He had started a book called *Lost Christian* and asked if I might skim his first chapter. Intrigued by the title, I said yes.

Back in my room, I turned on the light next to the bed and read his pages. His writing was funny at times and astonishingly transparent. But it also contained serious questions. Stacey had been in a "dark night of the soul" for a very long time. Though he practiced the trappings of his faith, a deep existential despair brewed inside. *Where is God? Does he love me specifically? Can I count on him? Can I ever really know him?* Those questions had tormented him for years, even decades.

Then in 2003, he was in a terrible car wreck. Numerous people gathered around him with prayer, love, and support. The incident clarified the severity of his dark spiritual struggle because he almost died. Yet the post-accident time was especially troublesome—so many prayed for him, but he still felt far from God. He continued to pray, attend church, and read the Bible, knowing the benefit of these actions but feeling the futility of them too. A growing discouragement hovered over Stacey because he didn't know God. What was worse, he didn't know *how* to know God.

I identified with his despair. Religion without any real experience of God feels pointless. Why try? Why even do all that stuff at church? Does it even matter?

Poring over his manuscript under the dim light in my room, I realized Stacey represented the audience I hoped to reach. He was not alone in his feelings. I've met many people in church who expressed the same confusion. Numerous authors, leaders, pastors, and teachers have written books about knowing God, but they rarely tell of any authentic experiences with him. The church at large does very little teaching about intimacy with God or how to connect with him in a real way.

How many believers have, like Stacey, reached a crisis of faith, weary of religious routines and appearances?

When Oswald Chambers was about Stacey's age, he had been conscious of God speaking personally to him only a few times. Biographer David McCasland wrote:

Once, when sitting in his room late one night, his collie, Tweed, had come in through the window, put his head on Oswald's knee, looked into his eyes for a few minutes, then gone out again.
Another time, his door opened and in came the baby boy of the house, barefoot and in his night-clothes. He came up to him and said, "Mr. Chambers, I loves you" and went back to his bed.
Again, while conducting a Christian Endeavour meeting, a mentally retarded girl walked down the church aisle and laid a bunch

of withered flowers on the table. A piece of paper tied to the flowers said, "With love from daft Meg." Each event seemed to be a tender touch from the Father conveying His presence and love.[1]

However, Chambers also wrote in his journal, "I was getting very desperate. I knew no one who had what I wanted; in fact I did not know what I did want. *But I knew that if what I had was all the Christianity there was, the thing was a fraud.*"[2]

A. W. Tozer, most known for his book *The Pursuit of God*, had the same longing for something real. He said,

> There is today no lack of Bible teachers…but too many of these seem satisfied to teach the fundamentals of the faith year after year, strangely unaware that there is in their ministry no manifest Presence…. They minister constantly to believers who feel within their breasts a longing which their teaching simply does not satisfy…. For it is not mere words that nourish the soul, but God Himself, and *unless and until the hearers find God in personal experience they are not the better for having heard the truth.*

Unless we find God in personal experience, teaching does not satisfy. He continued:

> The Bible is not an end in itself, but a means to bring men to an intimate and satisfying knowledge of God, that they may enter into Him, that they may delight in His Presence, may taste and know the inner sweetness of the very God Himself in the core and center of their hearts.[3]

Tozer yearned for God with an unquenchable thirst. He wouldn't settle for a mere inference, an ideal, or a benevolent creative force behind our existence. He believed God was knowable. He considered biblical men, like Moses, Isaiah, Elijah, and Paul, and others, like St. Francis, Martin Luther, Finney, and Thomas a Kempis. Though they were all different in personality and purpose, he saw something similar in their lives.

> The one vital quality which they had in common was spiritual receptivity. Something in them was open to heaven, something which urged them Godward.... They had spiritual awareness.... And they went on to cultivate it until it became the biggest thing in their lives. They differed from the average person in that when they felt the inward longing they *did something about it*. They acquired the lifelong habit of spiritual response.[4]

Tozer followed their example and consistently did something about it. He waited for God's presence. Lying face down on his office floor, he spent many hours in worship and prayer, soaking in God's love. And God did not disappoint him. The Lord still looks all throughout the earth, seeking those whose hearts are completely his.[5]

Tozer's words struck me...*spiritual receptivity...awareness...*and *cultivate*. These respected men of the past knew that God communicated in the present. As true followers of Jesus, they were aware. They paid attention, noticing things like dreams, impressions, visions, and the still small voice of the Holy Spirit. They cultivated their sensitivity—they *did something* about it.

If you don't believe it's possible in the first place, you won't pay attention. If you don't pay attention, you won't develop. It all comes down to faith—believing that God wants to be with you and talk to you, to show you the mystery and wonder of his ways. But more than that, he longs to tell you that you're loved, even adored.

I opened the door of my life to God when I was fourteen. Later I had to overcome the snare of religiosity, the lie of condemnation, and the exhausting Martha-like lifestyle. I had to admit I was mad at God for not running the world the way I wanted. I had to dismantle all the barriers that kept me far away from him. Soon after I did, I found a new spiritual receptivity and awareness.

Many people resist taking the initial step. They erect blockades around their hearts and then wonder why they feel distant from God. "I can't trust a God who would let 9/11 happen," a man said on TV. That's a choice. He put up a wall. Other barriers have been built by the Enemy from our original wounds. If we were hurt as children, we zealously guard our hearts, stringing yellow police tape around the crime scenes of our past. We choose safety. We keep God at arm's length. Yet God can take those hurts away if we're willing.

The first step is to trust.

When I read *The Sacred Romance* by Brent Curtis and John Eldredge, I wept through the entire book. Their honest stories answered my tight-fisted questions about whether God could be trusted or not, especially when it came to the pain and suffering of life. As I turned the last page and closed the book, the question was settled forever. Yes, there will be unjust suffering and difficult times ahead. I don't know what God will require of me or others I know and love. Even so, I decided I would trust God no matter what it looked like here on earth. God greatly values such faith, because trust is a prerequisite for intimacy. He confirmed this through an unusual sequence of events.

One day my friend Mary Jean told me about an accident involving a man named George. He had been riding his motorcycle and unexpectedly collided with a deer. The wreck was terrible, and doctors said he could be bedridden for life. The same day, Jenny called and mentioned that her friend Whitney had just died. Whitney contracted multiple sclerosis after her second child was born, and she deteriorated rapidly. The debilitating disease caused muscle weakness and mental confusion. Soon her husband made the difficult decision to put her in a rest home. He took their kids to visit her often. Nearly twenty years later, she finally died.

Something distressed me deep inside. *George* and *Whitney*.[6] Their names echoed in my head. Two wonderful people were inexorably shortchanged in life without any warning. Short of a miracle, their earthly realities were forever altered. I wrestled with the unfairness. As I lay in bed that night, I tossed and turned. As if I were chewing gristle, I couldn't break the problem down. Life seemed so randomly cruel. An hour went by. Finally, I turned to my heavenly Father, surrendering my restless thoughts. I know now that he was listening in those late night hours. "Call to Me," he said in Jeremiah, "and I will answer you, and I will tell you great and mighty things, which you do not know."[7] During the night I had a riveting dream.

In the dream I'm in an open grassy space of a wooded area, sitting at a large round table with five other friends. Giant redwood trees border the clearing. We are discussing George's situation. The mood is solemn. A few look down at their laps, and some cannot hold back their tears.

As usual, I'm taking notes on a yellow pad. I'm distraught too, but eager to devise some kind of plan to help George's family. We exchange our thoughts, yet for all our brainstorming, we don't have any brainy ideas.

Directly over us the clouds suddenly split. I know something supernatural is happening, because they're moving apart so fast. Blue sky highlights a heavenly portal above. Slowly, God's enormous right arm descends toward earth through the opening. He's pointing toward something. Our discussion stops abruptly. We all lean back in our chairs, staring up at the spectacle. I can barely breathe when I realize his arm is swinging down toward our exact location. His hand appears larger and larger the closer it comes.

Everything is hushed with awe. The wind is dead still, and the birds go silent. Gradually it dawns on me that God's finger has stopped precisely over the notepad where I'm hoping to record our grandiose ideas to fix George's shattered world. I almost flip backward in my chair but teeter in the balance, holding on to the table with my hand and my right leg extended. I know God is about to say something, and I'm seized up with expectancy. Then, in the absolute kindest voice I've ever heard, God speaks:

"IT'S NOT ABOUT THIS LIFE," he says, pausing for a moment.

"TAKE NOTE OF THAT."

The dream ended there. I woke up and replayed the scene in my mind's eye. His words were straightforward, bold, and perfectly clear. The kindness in his tone was disarming and will stay with me for rest of my life. God was not wringing his hands over George's tragedy. His voice was not anxious, apologetic, or annoyed. Implicit in his simple phrases was a pointed message: "Trust me, no matter what it looks like."

Eldredge and Curtis say that all our time on earth is a small story. We enter this world with a propensity to live life on our own terms and through our own understanding. But God is fiercely determined to disrupt our small stories. Our unseen Lover draws us, coaxes us, and even woos us with the message that we were designed for a much bigger story. That is the *sacred romance*[8] they wrote about in their wonderful book.

From my perspective, George and Whitney's earthly stories were catastrophic. God chose not to intervene. There were no miraculous healings, no happy endings. Yet this didn't mean that God was capricious or uncaring. His unconditional love stood firm and unwavering and will only be understood when we see the longer view.

If you could remember what it felt like to be a baby in the womb, you might complain about the umbilical-cord diet and cramped quarters, even though it's a cozy place. When the labor pains start, things aren't so pleasant any more. You can hear the doctors and nurses. Their muffled voices tell you there's a much bigger life awaiting you outside the safe space you've always known. You're not so sure. You want to hold on to what's familiar. The transition is terrifying.

But there's no stopping it now. You are being pushed by an invisible force. You have to go. You begin to panic. Squeezing through the dark tunnel, the sounds get louder at the end. The pressure builds. You don't think you can stand another minute. At last you break free into the room, breathe in the fresh, new air, and someone wraps you in a soft blanket. You open your eyes and faces smile down at you. Familiar, joyful voices are now clearer. You begin to warm up. This isn't all that bad after all. This new world is far more incredible than you ever imagined.

Death is like birth in this way. We hold on tightly to our own comfort, because we don't know God's love and his infinitely beautiful plans. Jesus said, "I go to prepare a place for you."[9] Paul wrote, "No eye has seen, no ear has heard, no mind has conceived what God has prepared for those who love him, but God has revealed it to us by his Spirit."[10] If you take God at his word, you can begin to see life on earth from an entirely different perspective. You can find something larger than your losses to live for.

The most important thing to learn in our fleeting time on earth is that we are God's beloved. You're his favorite, and so am I. His thoughts about us are more numerous than the grains of sand on all the beaches. He knows our minds and notices when we look to him. Even before we speak, he knows what we will say. He watches us all the time. He sees us in the dark and counts our hidden tears. He'll go to the ends of the earth to bring us into his embrace.[11]

"For God *so loved* the world." This is what God is like. He will say it many times and many ways, because it's so vital. He said it most profoundly by entering the human race, walking among us, teaching us about his kingdom, and ultimately, dying for us. But he'll also show you his love in tangible ways *right now.* Maybe you'll read a scripture that captures your heart, like Song of Solomon 7:10. Maybe the sound of worship music will open the heavens over your tired soul. Maybe you'll find a heart-shaped rock on a beach. Or maybe God will visit you in a movie or a dream.

One winter night, I was feverishly sick as I watched the film *Enchanted April* with my daughters. The movie was a good diversion from my throbbing head. I didn't know it would also stir my aching heart.

Based on Elizabeth Van Arnim's 1922 novel, the story is about four women in post–World War I England who rent a secluded castle in Italy.

They are disenchanted with life for different reasons, longing to be revived—body, mind, and soul.

I identified with the lady named Rose, a quiet person, barely functioning in a loveless marriage. Pain has killed her heart. Life in rainy, dreary England depicts the sorrow of her world.

In contrast, the beautiful Mediterranean Sea, the soft sunshine, and the fragrant flowers all create a perfect setting for refreshment and transformation. Slowly she unwinds. A smile returns to her face. She floats on her back in the sun-bathed water and comes back to life inside her soul. Eventually she invites her husband to join her there. He is enthralled with her beauty as if she's a woman he has never known. Her shimmering inner vitality has come alive.[12]

After the movie ended, I climbed into bed and noticed that the clock said 11:33. God reminded me of Jeremiah 33:11: "Yet, again, there shall be heard in this place…the voice of joy and the voice of gladness, the voice of the bridegroom and the voice of the bride, the voice of those who say, 'Give thanks to the LORD of hosts, for the LORD is good, for His lovingkindness is everlasting.'" Days before, God had given me this verse as a promise over my marriage. He assured me that joy would return to my life.

Watching Rose's restoration and her reconciliation to her husband dramatized this verse for me. God breathed life into my desolate, broken places. I fell asleep that night with hope in my heart and tears on my pillow.

That very night, God demonstrated his love even more dramatically through a dream. The setting is a vast, empty desert. Our friend Jack and his wife, Leesa, are sitting in our pickup truck on the edge of a sea of sand. The day is getting hotter by the minute. Apparently I have stepped out of the truck to give them more room. Leesa's window is open, so I lean on the door with my arms folded on the edge. We make casual conversation while Jack rests his arms on the steering wheel. Soon, I notice that he's staring at something straight ahead. I turn my face to check it out, shielding my eyes from the burning sun.

A tiny dot of a person is walking toward us. He is so far away that I squint to focus. He descends out of sight behind a sandy ridge but soon comes over the crest, still trudging in our direction. Dressed in an off-white robe, he looks like an Old Testament prophet. The rising heat over the desert makes him surreal and wavy. As he comes closer, I can see that he's weathered from the sun, his hair tousled from exposure, as if he's been walking a long time. We all watch his approach with fascination. When he's a dozen yards away, I let go of Leesa's window and stand up straight to greet him.

To my surprise, the man walks right up to me as if I'm the only one there. I take a step or two back, but he draws closer, his face only inches from mine. He gazes straight into my eyes, and I look into his without blinking. Held in the trance, my legs go weak, but I'm not afraid. There is something unspeakably wonderful about his face. I could tell him everything I've ever done—all my mistakes, all my negative thoughts, my compromises—and there would be no hint of shame. I know he would reach for my hands, and I imagine the comfort of his touch.

Then he speaks. "Do you know how God feels about you?"

"Well, I, uh…" I can't form a coherent sentence, as though my lips and tongue are numbed. His face, wrinkled by time, is so kind, but he doesn't exactly smile.

With gentle sincerity he asks me again. "Do you *know* how God feels about you?" His words vibrate with urgency, like nothing else matters until I know the answer to his question.

I look down with resignation. "I guess not…no, I'm not sure."

Immediately he steps forward and pulls me into his strong arms in a sweeping embrace. His left hand holds the back of my head and his right arm supports me. I lean back, limp in his arms, as he kisses my cheek. My knees give way. He holds me close, the side of his face touching mine for what seems like a long time. Every muscle, every cell of my being relaxes with one great sigh.

The scene faded away slowly and I awoke in my own bed, startled by the intensity of the dream. Tingling all over, I closed my eyes to feel the man's embrace again. For some reason, his gesture of affection didn't seem awkward or inappropriate. He was a person delivering a word from God. To experience God's embrace through this man's action was more powerful than any words.

I remember grabbing my young son in the kitchen, leaning his sweet little body back and kissing his face all over. He, too, melted in my arms, soaking in the adoration. I hugged all my children that way. Now they're all too tall for such embracing, but I feel the same passion for them. I wanted them to feel that love.

I understood what God was saying. As I wrote the details in my journal, the Holy Spirit brought a memory. I thought of the painting called "The Kiss," by Gustav Klimt. Years ago, my sister had a poster of it in her apartment. First exhibited in 1908, the original painting was extremely controversial, the image charged with eroticism. Of course in today's world, we're used to much worse. A painting of a fully dressed man kissing the cheek of a fully dressed woman is beautiful, even enchanting.

The painting embodies both the romantic love of a husband and wife, and the paternal love of a father for his child. Scripture uses both images to describe God's love for us. We are at once Christ's bride longing for her Bridegroom's embrace and the prodigal son who has returned to his father's arms. Either way, we win.

Soon after this dream, I came across Song of Solomon 2:6: "Let his left hand be under my head and his right hand embrace me." Could there have been a more exact description? The words expressed in detail the prophet-man's embrace in my dream and Klimt's painting. I could feel God's everlasting arms holding me. He laced it all together. The verse fit the context of what God had already said.

In the summer of 1930, Albert Einstein composed a piece he called "What I Believe." He concluded his credo with this statement:

The most beautiful emotion we can experience is the mysterious. It is the fundamental emotion that stands at the cradle of all true art and science. He to whom this emotion is a stranger, who can no longer wonder and stand rapt in awe, is as good as dead, a snuffed-out candle. To sense that behind anything that can be experienced there is something that our minds cannot grasp, whose beauty and sublimity reaches us only indirectly: this is religiousness. In this sense...I am a devoutly religious man.[13]

I concur with Einstein: to experience wonder and awe is synonymous with being alive. To know there is something greater behind it all is even better. But I think he missed the crux of the matter by believing God was unreachable and oblique. Michelangelo's painting on the ceiling of the Sistine Chapel depicts what some people believe—that God and man can never touch. Contact between heaven and earth is just out of reach.

But in my experience, I can say, "Not so!"

Knowing God personally is the pinnacle of life on earth. A breathtaking, beautiful possibility for all, and yet it's a mere appetizer in lieu of the coming feast in heaven.

You could be anywhere when life with God begins. If it hasn't begun yet, I hope this book is one of many things that jump-starts the connection. I hope these stories will be a catalyst that helps you recognize him in your world with all of its divine happenstance. God's voice may surprise you, but the texture of his words and his tone will be unmistakably about his love. Over time his love will fill up every empty space, every longing, every unmet need and deep loss inside you, and even overflow through you to other people. His love will be better than life itself.

And one day, you will know in your knowing place that God is utterly real, and no person, thing, or circumstance of life, tragic or otherwise, can ever take that away.

Epilogue
Wonders Never Cease

*I wish you would put the words in my mouth, God,
to tell the world what you're really like. Not a dead god who
lives in some building but a Father of kindness, a Son
of forgiveness, a Spirit who helps us...that's who you are.*
—KEVIN PROSCH, "HARP IN MY HEART," *PALANQUIN*

n the middle of what could be any major city in America, I find
myself standing in a small corner parking lot with about twenty people. The sun has descended to twilight.

I speak up, asking the group if they want to do the Hokey-Pokey
with me. A few chuckle, yet they seem willing. We form a circle and do
the dance, and afterward, somehow it seems like we're no longer strangers.

I hope to engage them, so I tell a joke. "I once saw a bumper sticker
at a truck stop that said, 'What if the Hokey-Pokey *is* what it's all
about?'" They laugh, listening now. I feel prompted by God to continue.
"But you know, there's so much more than the Hokey-Pokey," I say,
explaining that God is real and far beyond anything we've imagined.
"And the good news is that he wants to be known." Soon, I'm explaining the gist of the book you've just read.

By now, night has fallen and rush-hour traffic is making the city
noisy. I'm using my loudest voice, but I can't compete with the honking
horns, crowds on the sidewalks, and the roar of buses and cars. The people in the parking lot are huddled close, straining to hear.

I start to think, *Oh well, that's the best I can do,* when someone unexpectedly hands me a microphone. (I said to my editor, Mick Silva, that would be you.) I move over to a streetlight to continue, louder now and with a passion stirring inside. I use the simplest language I know. My words echo off the buildings. It's strange hearing my voice amplified, but for some reason, I'm not nervous or even self-conscious.

Many windows start to open on the tall buildings that surround the parking lot. People gather and some are even sitting on window sills. Vehicles pull over and double-park. The winter air is chilly, but people roll down their car windows anyway. I feel a connection with all who are listening. I'm surprised that they're remotely interested. Yet as I continue, I see their attentive faces and their bodies leaning in, trying not to miss a word. Maybe this is something they've wanted to hear for a very long time.

The dream ended there.

It was February 2006. I'd only written a few chapters of this book. The whole venture seemed like a long shot. The publishing world was daunting, and I had no idea how I'd even get in the door. But God encouraged me through this dream. So I kept writing. And eventually, to my surprise, it was published.

If these stories have touched you, I hope you will pass them on. I hope you will tell the circle of people standing in the parking lot of your life that there's so much more than the Hokey-Pokey, more than religion, more than even their biggest ideas of God.

God is not somewhere across the universe whirling in space. Rather, he's here, right now, closer than your skin.

Reading Group Guide

*See the complete expanded version of the Reading Group
Guide on www.closerthanyourskin.com*

CHAPTER ONE — FOLLOWING ALICE

Have you ever sensed a "sneeze" moment with God? See what you can
remember and share some of these experiences with your group. You
might want to start a "book of remembrance" to log your spiritual sneeze
moments with God.

CHAPTER TWO — BASIC TRUST

Picture yourself in a large room with God. What would he say to you?
What would you say to him? How far or close are you? Do you want to
embrace him or run? What parallels do you see to your experience of
your earthly father?

CHAPTER 3 — POINTS OF CONTACT

What helps you feel God's presence? How do you make time for those
things? Are there other ways you'd like to try to experience his presence?
You might consider reading some inspirational biographies (see
www.closerthanyourskin.com for ideas).

CHAPTER FOUR — LOVE CAME DOWN

Take time to think about how you first came to God. Share your
thoughts with your group. If you're not sure, share what you've experienced so far. Write out your faith journey to tell your story in your
own way.

CHAPTER 5 — GOT RELIGION?

Are your prayers ritualistic? Are you trying to do everything right spiritually? When you miss church, do you feel bad about yourself? Do you keep a scorecard on your spiritual activity? Do you do things to be noticed at church? Share your responses and check out Susan's Web site for the complete *Religiosity Self-assessment.*

CHAPTER 6 — NEVER GOOD ENOUGH

Have you experienced God in a personal way? Do you struggle with ongoing sin? Are you likely to give up something for Lent or make a New Year's resolution? Do you accept blame often? Do you apologize a lot? Share answers with your group and see the Web site for more.

CHAPTER SEVEN — EXPOSING MARTHA

Have you ever made an "inner vow?" Talk about a few of these in your group. Do you know how to rest? Is this problem worse for women than men? Share how this issue affects your own life, then read Luke 10:38-42 and discuss it together.

CHAPTER EIGHT — AMBUSHED BY LIFE

Why do bad things happen to good people? Have you put God on trial for causing you pain? A crisis can open doors for God to speak, or rather, for us to hear. Share an experience where you sensed God's comfort in a time of crisis.

CHAPTER NINE — INKLINGS

Do you believe you can know God intimately? Keep a journal to log special verses, dreams, coincidences, or impressions, and plan to share about any message God confirmed through two or more experiences the next time your group meets.

Chapter Ten — Puzzles

Discuss a biblical parable or metaphor that's significant to you (for example, gardening involves planting, pulling weeds, watering, pruning). Take turns interpreting how the metaphor relates to your lives and explain its meaning for your group.

Chapter Eleven — Thanksgiving.com

Do you tend to be optimistic or pessimistic? How has this shaped your view of God? Make a list of things you are thankful for, adding to it continually. Discuss any changes in your outlook the next time your group meets.

Chapter Twelve — Unwinding

Do you have a religious agenda—something you're doing for God? How do you think recognizing our "bankruptcy before God" changes one's faith? For the next week, start your day by asking God what He's doing today, and report to your group what happened.

Chapter Thirteen — Thoughts on Destiny

Desiring to help others and fix a broken world is natural and good. But if God's not in it, our labor is in vain. When you consider the specific purpose God created you for, is anything blocking you from that? Often, the supernatural, mysterious side of God can make us uncomfortable and cause us to struggle with trying to fix things on our own. Discuss the difference.

Chapter Fourteen — Anchored

Do you understand the term "silent divorce"? Share your views on some of the inherent spiritual challenges of marriage. Where do you feel most fulfilled? Does God factor in? Why is vulnerability so important in close relationships? Discuss with your group.

Chapter Fifteen — Repairing Desolations

Do you recognize any patterns of behavior in your life that echo an original wound? Have you seen others living out of their wounds? Share your observations. Read Matthew 18: 23–35 as a group and discuss practicing intentional forgiveness with those who have hurt you.

Chapter Sixteen — No Stones or Snakes

Does raising a child in today's world scare you? Discuss the struggle of ensuring they'll adopt your values. How does one set an example of authentic faith in hard times? In what ways can we teach them how God works through events in our lives?

Chapter Seventeen — Steadfast Love

How does one balance between an invasive, godless culture and an overprotective Christian bubble? Should we be honest with children about our own process of spiritual growth? Describe the ways we can share with children about how God answers and guides us.

Chapter Eighteen — Three Hammers

Have you experienced two-way conversation with God? Do specific prayers test God or are general prayers weak and less effective? Try reflexive prayer over the next week and pray about whatever comes up. Listen and let God lead you, then share your experiences with your group.

Chapter Nineteen — A Bald Man in Plaid

How can we tell the difference between heavenly and earthly wisdom? Read James 3:13–18 and discuss your responses. Patiently listen for what God says about you first, then ask him to give revelatory words of encouragement for other members of your group, consulting Scripture together (see Web site for more).

CHAPTER TWENTY — PSYCHIC CHRISTIANS?

Do you fear the enemy's power to deceive you? Discuss the safeguards in the chapter. Are there others you would add? The Holy Spirit always speaks in unison with Scripture, with love and hope, so read the Bible for yourself (and check out www.closerthanyourskin.com for more).

CHAPTER TWENTY-ONE — BELOVED

Do you sense a gap between knowing about God and actually knowing him? Is it hard to trust? If our stories are often short and tragic, how does that square with the larger story God is telling? Share about ways God has proven his love to you—maybe through a dream, a painting, or a scripture—weaving the message through numerous experiences.

If this book has helped you, if your heart has been stirred, keep learning. Be alert, for God has promised if we search for him with all our hearts, we will find him. Step into eternity with the One who calls you beloved forever.

—SUSAN

Acknowledgments

As a writer, I started out with something to say, but soon realized I needed to learn how to write. As a result, I have many friends to thank. Bill Buckley edited my first article. Claudia LeCoure invited me to a local writer's group. Kathy Tyers, Sharon Dunn, and Jenny Thornburg gave me valuable critiques and editing advice. Simon Presland worked with me online and set up a critique group. Both locally and online, I received much needed help from these new writing friends and others. Thank you one and all.

From my online group, I met Marilyn Tyner. She received permission to take Chapter Six and converted it into a tract that will be circulated in several prison systems. That moves my heart.

At Mount Hermon Writer's Conference, I found great writing teachers: Roger Palms, David Kopp, and most recently Cecil Murphey. Thank you for your wisdom, encouragement, and inspiration. I couldn't take notes fast enough.

Then one fine April afternoon, I met Mick Silva, my editor with WaterBrook. He took a chance on a new writer and a book only half-written. He understood what I wanted to say and cheered me on, shaping the result you now hold in your hands. He is an editor of the new-wine-skin variety, and I am grateful to him far beyond these few words.

In my life, I want to thank the Yates and the Andersons and the ministry of Young Life. You encouraged me in the early days of my faith. Also my Wednesday Group (aka "The Ladies Aid Society"), my Home Group (Donaldsons, Martinsons, Callahans, and Herreras), and the Gaskills, Thornburgs, Fremonts, Smiths, and the Mazzas: beyond my family, you are my community. My gratitude overflows to Jenny, for introducing me to the ways of the Holy Spirit...to my pastors, Dave Delgatty, James Tharp, and Chris Blackmore, for being good shepherds...to Jack Deere, for your friendship and the solid teaching of your books...and to Sharon Daines and Bible Study Fellowship for giving me a deep passion for the Bible.

My sister Nancy brought the gospel to me. I will never forget that beautiful blue-green day. To my wonderful parents, Richard and Carolyn, how can I thank you enough for the unconditional love you've given me all my life. Your love laid a spiritual foundation for what God is really like. I am doubly blessed to have had the same love from all four of my grandparents.

To my children, Katie (and John), Sarah, and Nate: in this time on earth, you are my joy. And to my husband Duncan: thank you for persevering in marriage. Thank you for believing in this venture and undergirding me in my self-doubt and weariness. But most of all, without you, there wouldn't be a book. Thank you for taking me by the hand and saying, "There's more to knowing God...and we're going to find him."

And finally, I want to acknowledge God. In the words of my daughter, Sarah, when she was two:

"God, I thank you for God, because he gives 'the happy' in all these rooms."

Notes

PROLOGUE

1. A. W. Tozer, *The Pursuit of God* (Camp Hill, PA: Christian Publications, 1948). Jack S. Deere, *Surprised by the Power of the Spirit* (Wheaton, IL: Zondervan, 1993). Jack S. Deere, *Surprised by the Voice of the God* (Wheaton, IL: Zondervan, 1996). John Ortberg, *God Is Closer Than You Think: This Can Be the Greatest Moment of Your Life Because This Moment Is the Place Where You Can Meet God* (Wheaton, IL: Zondervan, 2005).
2. Job 33:14 (unless otherwise noted, all Scripture comes from the New American Standard Version [NASB], 1995).
3. Jeremiah 29:13–14.

CHAPTER 1 FOLLOWING ALICE

1. Mike Mason, *Practicing the Presence of People: How We Learn to Love* (Colorado Springs: WaterBrook Press, 1999), 14.
2. John 10:27.
3. See Genesis 35:14; Joshua 4:9; 24:26; 1 Samuel 7:12.

CHAPTER 2 BASIC TRUST

1. Matthew 6:9.
2. See Genesis 17:1; Exodus 14:21; Exodus 13:21–22.
3. Mark 14:36.
4. Anna Dostoevsky, *Dostoevsky: Reminiscences,* trans. Beatrice Stillman (New York: Liveright, 1975), 147.

5. Liubov Fedorovna Dostoevskaia, *Fyodor Dostoevsky: A Study* (London: W. Heinemann, 1921), 274.

6. Bill Glass with Terry Pluto, *Champions for Life: The Healing Power of a Father's Blessing* (Deerfield Beach, FL: Faith Communications, Health Communications, 2005), 18–19, 35.

7. Donald Miller, *Blue Like Jazz: Nonreligious Thoughts on Christian Spirituality* (Nashville: Thomas Nelson, 2003), 4.

8. Donald Miller and John MacMurray, *To Own a Dragon: Reflections on Growing Up Without a Father* (Colorado Springs: NavPress, 2006).

9. Laura Ingalls Wilder, *On the Banks of Plum Creek,* rev. ed. (New York: Harper & Row, 1953), 33–34, italics mine.

CHAPTER 3 POINTS OF CONTACT

1. Lyrics by Phillips Brooks, music by Lewis H. Redner, "O Little Town of Bethlehem," *Christmas Songs and Easter Carols* (New York: E. P. Dutton & Company, 1903).

2. Lyrics by Placide Cappeau de Roquemaure, music by Adolphe Charles Adam, trans. John Sullivan Dwight, "O Holy Night," Carols Old and Carols News, (Boston: Parish Choir, 1916), #741.

3. Isaiah 55:8.

4. Brother Lawrence, *The Practice of the Presence of God* (Grand Rapids, MI: A Spire Book, Fleming H Revell, Baker Book House, 1958, 1967), 15.

5. Albert Schweitzer, *Memoirs of Childhood and Youth,* trans. C. T. Campion (New York: MacMillan, 1924), 52.

6. Philip Yancey, *Disappointment with God* (Grand Rapids, MI: Zondervan, 1988), 281–83.

7. Anne Fremantle, "Introduction to Fyodor Dostoevsky: The Grand Inquisitor," Researching The Brothers Karamazov (New York: Ungar, 1956), http://www.dartmouth.edu/~karamazo/ fremantle.html, 3.

8. Fremantle, "Introduction to Fyodor Dostoevsky," 4.

9. Fyodor Dostoevsky, *The Brothers Karamazov,* trans. and anno-
tated Richard Pevear and Larissa Volokhonsky (New York:
Farrar, Straus and Giroux, 1990), 249.

10. Matthew 7:7.

Chapter 4 Love Came Down

1. Dag Hammarskjöld, *Markings* (New York: Alfred A. Knopf,
1964), 48.

2. Information taken from www.passion-play.com (accessed 2
August 2007).

3. Mike Mason, *The Mystery of Marriage* (Sisters, OR: Mult-
nomah, 1985, 2005), 43.

Chapter 5 Got Religion?

1. Leo Tolstoy, taken from
www.brainyquote.com/quotes/quotes/l/leotolstoy153590.html
(accessed 2 August 2007).

2. Chris Welsh, *Repetoire* [*sic*] *CD bio-notes,* www.spiritinthesky
.com/reviews.htm (accessed 2 August 2007).

3. Author unknown, "Hunky and Dory and The Kingdom of Food,"
www.gnte.org/ecopub/hunkyand.htm (accessed 6 March 2007).

4. See Revelation 3:20; 2:2–4.

Chapter 6 Never Good Enough

1. John 8:11.

2. Oswald Chambers, *My Utmost for His Highest: An Updated Edi-
tion in Today's Language* (Grand Rapids, MI: Discovery House,
1992), January 1 and March 11 entries.

3. Mark Twain, *Personal Recollections of Joan of Arc* (New York:
Nelson Doubleday, published by arrangement with Harper &
Row, 1922), 325–26.

4. Mark Swett, "Waco Never Again," Branch Davidians, Waco, and the FBI, *Apologetics Index,* www.apologeticsindex.org/b10.html# theology (accessed 2 August 2007); James Trimm, "A Doctrine Unto Death: Branch Davidian Theology," *The Watchman Expositor,* vol. 11, no. 4, 1994, www.watchman.org/cults/fagan.htm (accessed 2 August 2007).

5. Marvin Olasky, "A Cold War for the 21st Century," *World Magazine,* November/December 2001, 20.

6. See 1 John 4:18; Ephesians 1:5, 7; 2:10; Hebrews 12:2, 5–10.

7. Philip Yancey, *Disappointment with God* (Grand Rapids, MI: Zondervan, 1988).

8. *Blood Diamond,* directed by Edward Zwick (Burbank, CA: Warner Bros., 2006).

9. 1 John 3:1 (NIV).

Chapter 7 Exposing Martha

1. John Loren Sandford and Paula Sandford, *The Transformation of the Inner Man* (Tulsa, OK: Victory House, 1982), 191–205.

2. *Saving Private Ryan,* directed by Steven Spielberg (CITY: DreamWorks SKG, Paramount Pictures, and Amblin Entertainment, 1998).

3. *Papillon,* directed by Franklin J. Schaffner (Burbank, CA: Allied Artists, Warner Bros., 1973).

4. See Luke 10:38–41.

Chapter 8 Ambushed by Life

1. Proverbs 14:10; 15:13.

2. John Loren Sandford and Paula Sandford, *The Relationship Series on Video,* "Getting to Know You: How We See Each Other" (Post Falls, ID: Elijah House, 1993).

3. Prologue contains the detailed story.

4. J. D. Salinger, *Franny and Zooey* (New York: Little, Brown and Co., 1989), 68.

5. Catherine Marshall, *Something More* (New York: Avon Books, 1974), 39.

6. Marshall, *Something More,* 33–51.

7. See Matthew 18:21–35.

Chapter 9 Inklings

1. Words by Thomas O. Chisholm, music by William M. Runyon, "Great Is Thy Faithfulness," (Carol Stream, IL: Hope, 1923, renewal 1951).

2. For more on this topic, see *Spiritual Moments with the Great Hymns,* Evelyn Bence (Grand Rapids, MI: Zondervan, 1977).

3. Genesis 18:14.

4. Isaiah 54:6.

5. Exodus 3:3–4 (NIV).

6. See Matthew 13:11–12.

7. Job 33:14.

Chapter 10 Puzzles

1. See Mark 4:2–20.

2. Stephen Strang, "He Who Has Ears…," *Charisma,* April 1996, 84.

3. Mark 4:9, 23.

Chapter 11 Thanksgiving.com

1. Psalm 116:15.

2. *Hope Floats,* Fortis Films, Twentieth Century-Fox Film Corp., 1998.

3. *The Lilac Blooms: The Story of Milaina and a Tribute to the Faithfulness of God.* For the complete story, contact Ron and Nell Baar at ronandnell@hotmail.com.

4. Psalm 69:20, 29, 30–32.

5. See John 14:26.

6. C. S. Lewis, *Reflections on the Psalms* (New York: Harcourt, Brace & World, 1958), 93.

7. See Psalm 100:4.

CHAPTER 12 UNWINDING

1. David McCasland, *Oswald Chambers: Abandoned to God* (Grand Rapids, MI: Discovery House, 1993), 258.

2. Job 33:14–17.

3. Matthew 5:30.

4. Harriet Beecher Stowe, *Uncle Tom's Cabin* (New York: Harper & Row, 1958), 53.

5. Proverbs 3:5.

6. See Psalm 127:1.

7. See John 15:5.

8. See 2 Corinthians 10:4–5.

9. James 2:14, 20, 18.

10. See John 21:1–7.

11. Oswald Chambers, *My Utmost for His Highest* (Toronto: McClelland and Stewart, Ltd., Dodd, Mead, 1935), August 30 entry.

12. Albert Schweitzer, *Memoirs of Childhood and Youth* (New York: Macmillan, 1949), 67–68.

13. C. S. Lewis, *Mere Christianity* (New York: Macmillan, Collier Books, 1943), 127.

CHAPTER 13 THOUGHTS ON DESTINY

1. See John 15:1–11.

2. See John 5:19.

3. Benedikt Taschen, *Van Gogh,* trans. Michael Hulse, Cologne (edited and produced by Ingo F. Walther, Rainer Metzger, 1996), 18.

4. Taschen, *Van Gogh,* 17.

5. David McCasland, *Oswald Chambers: Abandoned to God* (Grand Rapids, MI: Discovery House, 1993), 53.

6. McCasland, *Abandoned to God*, 55.

7. Revelation 12:1–4.

8. The full story is in Chapter 1.

CHAPTER 14 ANCHORED

1. From a speech given at a prayer conference by Francis Frangipane, Helena, Montana, 1997. Used with permission.

2. See John 12:24; 1 Corinthians 15:31.

3. *Contact,* directed by Robert Zemeckis (Burbank, CA: Warner Bros., 1997).

CHAPTER 15 REPAIRING DESOLATIONS

1. See Exodus 34:7; Deuteronomy 5:9.

2. Isaiah 61:4.

3. Isaiah 62:4.

4. See Deuteronomy 11:26–28, for example.

5. Taken from www.texasfreeway.com/Dallas/photos/i35w/i35w.shtml.

6. For more information on "safe talk" see the Reading Group Guide.

7. Most of this teaching comes from John Loren Sandford and Paula Sandford, *The Transformation of the Inner Man* (Tulsa: Victory House, 1982); and Edward M. Smith, *Genuine Recovery* (Campbellsville, KY: Alathia, 1997).

8. Luke 23:34.

9. See Malachi 2:13–15; Matthew 5:22–24; 1 John 2:9; 4:20–21.

CHAPTER 16 NO STONES OR SNAKES

1. Dale Hanson Bourke, *Everyday Miracles* (Irving, Texas: Word, 1989), later published as "Motherhood—It Will Change Your Life," *Guideposts,* May 1990, 13–14.

2. Isaiah 30:20–21.

3. Matthew 7:9–11.

4. For biblical references in the paragraph read Genesis 16:13; Psalm 6:9; Job 37:13; 37:16; 38:36; and Jeremiah 33:3.

5. Isaiah 49:15–16.

Chapter 17 Steadfast Love

1. Article unavailable. Frank Peretti referenced with permission.

2. C. S. Lewis, *Reflections on the Psalms* (New York: Harcourt, Brace & World, 1958), 57.

3. Gary Phillips, "A Tale of Two Sons," *Kindred Spirit,* Dallas Theological Seminary, summer 1991.

4. Albert Schweitzer, *Memoirs of Childhood and Youth* (New York: Macmillan, 1949), 55.

5. Schweitzer, *Memoirs,* 42–43.

6. See Matthew 16:19; 12:29; Mark 3:27.

7. *Home Alone,* directed by Chris Columbus (Libertyville, IL: Hughes Entertainment, Twentieth Century Fox Film Corp., 1990).

8. Isaiah 44:2–5.

Chapter 18 Three Hammers

1. Mark Twain, *Personal Recollections of Joan of Arc* (New York: Nelson Doubleday, Inc., 1922), 112.

2. *World Book Medical Encyclopedia,* Rush-Presbyterian-St. Luke's Medical Center, 1998, 750.

3. See Psalm 89:14.

4. Matthew 5:44.

5. See Genesis 18:16–33.

6. See 2 Corinthians 4:18; Colossians 1:16;. Hebrews 11:1, 3.

7. "A Prayer Meeting that Lasted 100 Years," ChristianityToday. com, January 1, 1982, http://ctlibrary.com/3263 (accessed 2 August 2007).

8. "Moravians (religion)," Wikimedia Foundation, *Wikipedia,*
   http://en.wikipedia.org/wiki/Moravian_Brethren (accessed 2
   August 2007).

9. See Mark 4:23–25.

10. See James 1:22–25.

11. 1 Samuel 23:2.

12. See Malachi 2:13–16.

13. See Luke 11:9–12; James 4:2

14. See John 11:1–45; Luke 11:9–12; Hebrews 11:6.

15. See Luke 11:5–8.

16. Nehemiah 1:4.

17. Phil Elliston, sermons given at Christian Center, Bozeman,
    Montana, 2005.

18. John 10:27.

Chapter 19 A Bald Man in Plaid

1. See Jeremiah 33:3; James 1:5; 3:17.

2. 1 Corinthians 2:4–5, 13.

3. Isaiah 51:12–16.

4. Galatians 6:1, 3.

5. See Matthew 1:20.

6. See Genesis 41.

7. Ezekiel 33:6.

8. John 4:29.

9. Acts 2:17–18; see also Joel 2:28–29.

Chapter 20 Psychic Christians?

1. All information in the opening story comes from Rebecca Lee, "The
   Jerusalem Syndrome," *The Atlantic Monthly,* May 1995, 24–38.

2. Mark 5:15.

3. Taken from http://news.yahoo.com/s/ap/20061024/
   ap_on_re_us/ohio_execution.

4. Taken from http://news.yahoo.com/s/nm/20061024/us_nm/ execution_ohio_dc_1.

5. John 10:27.

6. John 16:12–13.

7. Acts 10:13.

8. Acts 5:35–39.

9. Matthew 11:4–5.

10. Matthew 7:15–16, 20.

11. See John 8:3–11.

12. Luke 9:54–56.

13. Alan Lightman, *Einstein's Dreams* (New York: Pantheon Books/Random House and simultaneously Toronto: Alfred A. Knopf, 1993), www.dr-dream.com/hist.htm; and *Streams 101*, a course on dreams and visions by John Paul Jackson, Streams Ministries International.

14. See Exodus 8:5–7.

15. Merrill F. Unger, *The New Unger's Bible Dictionary*, rev. ed. (Chicago: Moody Press, 1988), 313.

16. Wikimedia Foundation, *Wikipedia*, "Numerology," http://en.wikipedia.org/wiki/Numerology (accessed 2 August 2007).

17. Taken from http://www.tribute.ca/prn_synop.asp?m_id=13421.

Chapter 21 Beloved

1. David McCasland, *Oswald Chambers: Abandoned to God* (Grand Rapids, MI: Discovery House, 1993), 82.

2. McCasland, *Oswald Chambers*, 82, italics mine.

3. A. W. Tozer, *The Pursuit of God*, legacy ed., (Camp Hill, PA: Christian Publications, 1982, 1993), 8–9, italics mine.

4. Tozer, *Pursuit of God*, 63.

5. See 2 Chronicles 16:9.

6. Names changed to protect identity.

7. Jeremiah 33:3.

8. Brent Curtis and John Eldredge, *The Sacred Romance: Drawing Closer to the Heart of God* (Nashville: Thomas Nelson, 1997), XX.

9. John 14:2.

10. 1 Corinthians 2:9–10, NIV.

11. Psalm 139 is one of many references for these thoughts.

12. *Enchanted April,* directed by Mike Newell (CITY?: Paramount Pictures, 1992).

13. Walter Isaacson, "Einstein & Faith," *Time,* April 5, 2007, 47, http://www.time.com/time/magazine/article/0,9171,1607298-2,00.html (accessed 2 August 2007), quoting from Albert Einstein, "What I Believe," 1930. See also www.sfheart.com/einstein.html.

About the Author

SUSAN D. HILL is an award-winning feature writer and a leader of interdenominational women's groups where she has sought answers to the common longing for a more authentic spiritual experience. She serves as administrator and on the board of the Uganda Orphans Fund, a nonprofit relief organization building orphan homes for victims of AIDS and war founded by her husband. Susan and her husband, Duncan, have three children and live in Montana.

"I was driving one day and Jimmy Needham's song 'Dearly Loved' came on the radio. When I heard it, I almost pulled over. His song is the central message of this book. Go to his Web site and check out 'Dearly Loved.' You're going to love it. His new album *SPEAK* is the launch of much more to come from this talented artist."

—SUSAN

You can learn more about Jimmy Needham through his Web site, www.jimmyneedham.com.

And be sure and check out www.closerthanyourskin.com to:

- share your own points of contact with God, and read about others' experiences
- check out the resource guide to learn about "safe talk" from chapter 15 or information on biblical dream interpretation
- download the expanded reading group guide
- find extra photos and details from the book
- get that blueberry cobbler recipe from Chapter Eleven
- and much more!